Women of the FRONTIER

Women of the FRONTIER

BILLY KENNEDY

AMBASSADOR INTERNATIONAL
Greenville, South Carolina • Belfast, Northern Ireland

Women of the Frontier

Printed in the United States of America
British spellings used throughout book

Cover design & page layout by A & E Media — Paula Shepherd

ISBN 1 932307 02 8

Published by the Ambassador Group

Ambassador Emerald International
427 Wade Hampton Blvd.
Greenville, SC 29609
USA
www. emeraldhouse.com

and

Ambassador Publications Ltd.
Providence House
Ardenlee Street
Belfast BT6 8QJ
Northern Ireland
www. ambassador-productions.com

The colophon is a trademark of Ambassador

*This book is dedicated to my loving wife Sally,
my daughter Julie and my parents*

The Lord is my Shepherd, I shall not want. He maketh me to lie down in green pastures; He leadeth me beside the still waters. He restoreth my soul; He leadeth me in the paths of righteousness for His name's sake.

Psalms 23, verses 1-3

List of Contents

Admiration for Women of True Grit

HUMAN ENDURANCE on the American frontier in the 18th and early 19th centuries is perhaps beyond the comprehension and the imagination of those of us living in the comfortable modern society of the early 21st century.

The settlement of a vast wilderness and the creation of a civilisation in what today has become the most powerful, most democratic and free nation in the world is undoubtedly one of the epic stories in global history and, at every opportunity, there should be fulsome recognition of a courageous people who were not deterred by the personal hardships and tragedies that they faced.

Settling the American frontier may have a romantic ring to it, perpetuated by the images created in the Hollywood western movies, but there was a starkness about life in the vast territories which the European immigrant settlers encountered in their long overland treks that were far from cosy and glamorous.

Indeed, at a time when travel and accessibility was very difficult, and at times hazardous and extremely dangerous, it is incredible just how much territory was settled, and in such a short span of years.

Many trekked long journeys on foot, while the others managed to move on horseback, either alone or as part of a train of Conestoga wagons.

Researching in the United States and at home in Northern Ireland for my books in the Scots-Irish Chronicles, I have come across some incredible stories of men and women who lived through wars, famine, disease and drought and survived to secure a firm foothold on land that was to be theirs and their families for generations and centuries to come.

The men were in the vanguard of the great march West over a century and a half, from the eastern seaboard states of New England through the Appalachian territories, and beyond the Mississippi River over the Rockies to the Pacific Ocean in the West and to Texas in the South.

Women, too, were an integral part of the onward journey by the hardy settlers through dense forests and over mountains in the Appalachians to the great plains of the south and west and their contribution to the frontier settlements as the backbone of the home, the community and the church was far-reaching.

I never cease to marvel at the extraordinary tenacity and the true grit of the wonderful womenfolk of the American frontier, in facing the awesome and grinding challenges of largely hitherto uninhabited lands, variable climates and a dangerously hostile environment that resulted in many lost lives.

They encountered a life of constant toil, home-making, child-minding and subservience that could not have been easy or even tolerable by the standards that we all come to expect today in our modern society.

But with love and care they ensured that family life became paramount, and the values that uphold society prospered.

The gallant women of the American frontier deserve our total admiration and plaudits, and in this book it has been my privilege to recount for posterity the deeds and the actions of a number of these heroines.

—*Billy Kennedy*

Foreword from America

THIS IS THE EIGHTH VOLUME written by Billy Kennedy, on the subject of the contributions and influence of the Scotch-Irish (Scots-Irish) in the development of the United States of America. Interesting, titillating and people-orientated, these books have awakened a latent interest on both sides of the Atlantic in the colorful, admirable and legendary Scots-Irish people who wielded an incredible influence over our culture, our history and our heritage.

It is not unexpected that almost all of the folks mentioned in Billy's previous volumes were men. This is not to suggest that he was favoring the male sex; rather, it is because our culture, for various and complex reasons, was generally not such as to allow women to assume roles of leadership, power or prominence.

So, Billy, in his previous books, has focused mostly on the histories and accomplishments of the Scots-Irish men folk: among them Sam Houston, Davy Crockett and Presidents Andrew Jackson, Andrew Johnson and James Knox Polk.

Nevertheless, there were women, both notable and unknown, who contributed incalculably to the development of our culture, heritage, and the course of our nation. Now, with this latest book, *Women of the*

Frontier, Billy Kennedy rescues these women from historical obscurity and shows the vital roles that they played in the conquering of the American frontier.

There is 15-year-old Rebecca Calhoun, found hiding in the woods after the bloody Long Cane massacre of February 1, 1760; later becoming the wife of Revolutionary War general Andrew Pickens, she was forced to take her children and abandon her home to avoid hostile Indians and British Tory forces. Rebecca's sister Anne, captured by Cherokee Indians during the 1760 attack, was later reunited with her family and reared six children.

Billy tells us the story of Rebecca Meek Kennedy, widowed but stalwart, who migrated from Londonderry to North Carolina with seven of her children, eventually settling at White's Fort (present-day Knoxville!).

He tells us about Ann Hennis Bailey, who also found herself widowed when her militiaman husband was killed in a Revolutionary War battle. In order to survive in the hostile frontier of the late 1700s, Ann adopted men's clothing and became a locally-renowned frontier scout, messenger, spy and Indian fighter.

These stories that Billy shares richly convey the tenacity, the pragmatism and the fortitude of our maternal forebears.

The question may be argued as to whether our friend Billy Kennedy should be praised and congratulated for devoting this eighth Scots-Irish book to women, or whether we should mildly chastise him, for "waiting so long" to do so. But we'll go with the congratulatory version and thank Billy for recognizing our womenfolk who worked so tirelessly, lovingly and relentlessly for their families and their country.

It would be good if this book creates as much reverberating interest on the subject as Billy's other books have done. It inspires only a few to take up the subject of the heretofore unrecognized influence of our maternal kin and if these few pursue the subject in a substantive and passionate way, then this book will have served its purpose.

It goes without saying that the women's contribution in moulding and shaping the character of their sons and daughters in America cannot be overstated. President Abraham Lincoln, for example, is quoted as saying: "All I have and all I hope to be, I owe it my mother."

Thanks, Billy, for rousing such a keen interest in those to whom we owe so much.

—*John Rice Irwin*

Founder, Director and Trustee of Museum of Appalachia (Norris, Tennessee)

* Dr. John Rice Irwin is Founder, Director and trustee of the Museum of Appalachia at Norris, Tennessee, 15 miles from the city of Knoxville. The extensive East Tennessee farm village has gained national and international recognition for its concentration on the rich culture and folklore in the Appalachian mountain region. Dr. Irwin has been a teacher, farmer, businessman, historian, and author. His wide range of interests also extends to the music of his south eastern home region. His family roots extend to Scots-Irish and Welsh immigrants who settled in the Appalachian region in the 18th century.

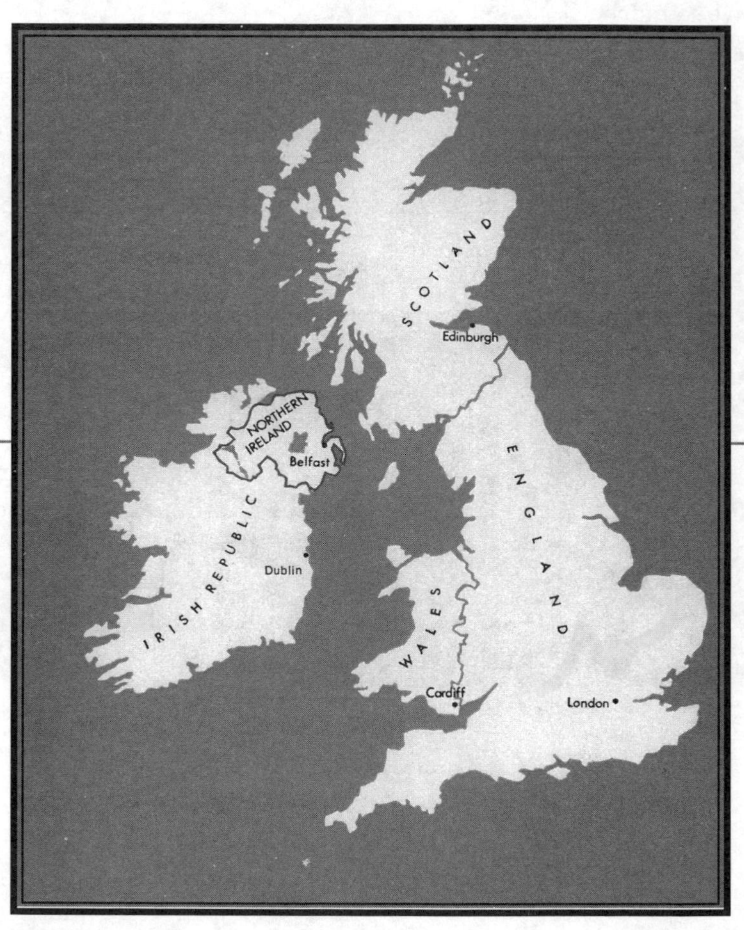
SCOTLAND
Edinburgh
NORTHERN IRELAND
Belfast
IRISH REPUBLIC
Dublin
ENGLAND
WALES
Cardiff
London

Foreword from Northern Ireland

IN HIS PREVIOUS BOOKS of the Scots-Irish Chronicles series, Billy Kennedy has outlined the important part played by the Scotch-Irish in the American Revolution, in the shaping of the old frontier and in the political leadership of the United States of America.

In this new book he outlines the lasting contribution of women to the American scene and their broad imprint on the American landscape and way of life.

It has been said that all-in-all, the middle colonies were the most significant cultural nursery of North America, because of the hybridisation of the various cultural groups who were attracted to Pennsylvania, the southern and western tiers of which the Scots-Irish largely fashioned and which became in turn the cradle of the Middle-West.

Billy Kennedy has already told the story of how the family farm and the family Bible were the foundations of faith. He now shows us how the dignity of the individual was so valued and how distinctions of class were so scorned that women could achieve in society that position which was denied them in the European homelands.

The cultural landscape of a large part of the present United States is still characterised by the single homestead and the unincorporated hamlet and by a corn and livestock economy which was pioneered in the Old West by the Scotch-Irish.

The success of the Scotch-Irish in frontier life was predicated by home life in the north of Ireland (Ulster) itself. There they had already been accustomed to living in rectangular houses with a wide-open hearth fitted with familiar gear such as crane and iron pots, flesh-hooks and pot-hooks, griddle and frying pan.

In America, Indian corn became a prolific substance for oats and barley and like them it was spring-sown and food for men and beast alike. Frontier clothing of leather and rawhide would have been no novelty to the Ulster immigrant, nor would Indian music consisting of drum and flute have been unfamiliar to them. They did indeed become more Cherokee than the Cherokees.

The Scotch-Irish were descended from the most ancient of peoples of the British Isles, the Picts and Scots. They took with them the heritage of farming and frontier life which had been learned through thousands of years at the Atlantic ends of Europe.

Their original society was matriarchal, their lineage matrilineal, until conquests by Indo-European groups such as the Celts and Anglo-Saxons. The American frontier women were re-empowered by the old ideals of freedom and democracy which became the hallmarks of the American people.

I believe this book will have a wide readership for I am convinced it is Billy Kennedy's best to date.

—*Dr. Ian Adamson OBE*
Belfast City Councillor

*Dr. Ian Adamson is a Belfast City Councillor, a member of the board of the Ulster-Scots Agency, a former Lord Mayor of Belfast, and a member of the Northern Ireland Assembly. He is the author of various historical books on Ulster. Books by Dr. Ian Adamson: *The Cruthin* (1974), *Bangor: Light of the World* (1979), *The Battle of Moira* (1980), *The Identity of Ulster* (1982), *The Ulster People* (1991), *William and the Boyne* (1995), *Dalaradia: Kingdom of the Cruthin* (1998).

Pathway to the Frontier

Stand at the Cumberland Gap and watch the procession of civilisation pass by marching single file: the buffalo following the trail; the salt springs the Indian, the fur trader and the hunter, the cattle raiser, the pioneer farmer, and the frontier has passed by.

—Frederick Jackson Turner.

1

Role of Women in a Men's World

ALEXANDER HAMILTON, Treasury Secretary in the first United States Administration under President George Washington, said in 1791 that manufacturing should be encouraged as a way to make use of "idle women and children" and thus improve the national economy.

It was a remarkable statement that brought a largely uncritical response in the strongly male chauvinist society of late 18th century America and the world at large.

Many women were prominently involved in the American Revolution, but it was very much a man's world in those days on crucial matters of politics and decision-making, and in the various facets of civic life.

Thomas Jefferson, a leading Revolutionary politician, did, however, radically propose in the draft Virginia Declaration of Rights that in "descents" or inheritances "females should have equal rights with males." But in the real decision-making it was the men who were always in the forefront.

All of the 56 signatures of the American Declaration of Independence of July 4, 1776 were of men and such was the accepted tradition in those days that it would have been unthinkable for women to be called to add their names to such a document, or indeed hold office in the Philadelphia legislature.

The reference in the Declaration which asserted: "We hold these truths to be self-evident, that men are created equal," was a cause of much conflict in the campaigns for women's rights in the United States and frequently alternative versions of the document were published.

The Senaca Falls Convention of 1848 stated: "We hold these truths to be self-evident, that all men and women are created equal."

Women did play an important role in many facets of the Revolutionary struggle.

They organised Revolutionary War boycotts of English goods and they made the wearing of home-spun cloth a patriotic duty and coffee was drunk rather than tea in the homes of the American patriotic classes.

Patriot pamphlets had female editors and a number of women were called into military action when the emergency demanded, some in very heroic circumstances when their husbands were killed or wounded or when enemy forces (native American tribes, the British or the French!) were in the ascendancy in a city or town.

On the frontier, women acted as scouts and spies for the patriot army and, operating from the cover of the indigenous communities, they were a real thorn in the side of British colonialist forces.

When the new American nation emerged, women were given the vote in only one state: New Jersey. But even this right was rescinded in 1807. Over a century was to elapse before women would have a more recognisable and sustainable place in American society.

2

Mary Polly (Finlay) Crockett

TENNESSEE FRONTIERSMAN'S WIFE

THE MOTHER of pretty Mary Polly Finlay (Finley), a Scots-Irish lass from East Tennessee, had ambitions that her daughter would marry a husband more settled and of greater substance than the intrepid David (Davy) Crockett who was keeping her company.

Polly's love, however, for this highly colourful and courageous frontiersman overcame her mother's doubts and, in a short but reasonably happy marriage which lasted almost ten years (1806-15), the couple flitted from various homes, through East and into Middle and West Tennessee.

Polly's parents were both of Scots-Irish immigrant families and her father William had been on expeditions with Daniel Boone in the Carolinas and Kentucky.

From first sight, Davy, who had earlier courted another young woman Margaret Elder, was in love with Polly and he admitted that he was "well pleased with her from the word go."

David was 20 and Polly a few years younger when they married on a license issued in Dandridge courthouse in East Tennessee on August 12, 1806 and the marriage was solemnised a few days later by a preacher after a few traditional frontier customs were observed.

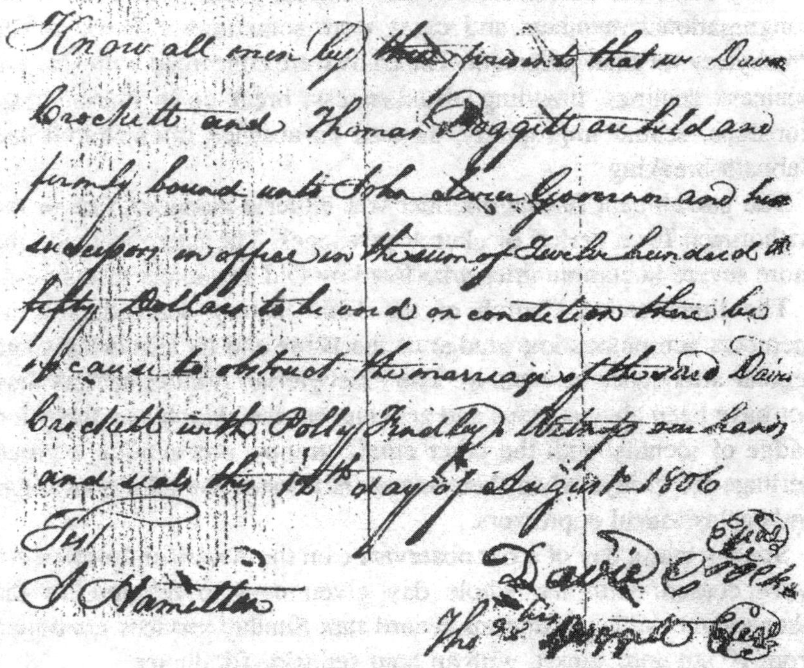

Marriage Bond

David Crockett and Polly Finley-August 12, 1806

Know all men by these presents that we David Crockett and Thomas Doggett are held and firmly bound unto John Sevier Governor and his successors in office in the sum of twelve hundred and fifty Dollars to be void on condition there be no cause to obstruct the marriage of the said David Crockett with Polly Findley. Witness our hands and seals this 12th day of August 1806

Test
J. Hamilton

David Crockett (Seal)
Thos his Doggett (Seal)

Davy's brothers and a few friends approached the Finlay home on his behalf with an empty jug. If Polly's father filled it up, this was the sign that he approved of the marriage and to Davy's delight the match was made when his friends came back with a pitcher overflowing. A wedding gift was two cows with calves.

The Crockett marriage produced three children: John Wesley, William, and Margaret Polly Finlay. But life was exceedingly difficult in the wooded wilderness of the Tennessee frontier for frail and delicate Polly.

Davy was for ever roaming the Tennessee forests and the mountains, leaving Polly alone for long periods with the children. It was a lonely, at times bleak existence in the rural hills of Tennessee in the early 19th century.

For the first few years of the marriage, they lived on a small rented farm at Bay's Mountain in Jefferson County, East Tennessee near the Finlay's Spring settlement of Polly's father, but they struggled to make end's meet and Davy was convinced their best hope was to move west to more fertile land.

Polly, it was said, kept a comfortable home within the meagre means and David could at least feed her and the children from his hunting in the forests and rivers, but there was little or no money to pay the rent, much less for the bare necessities of a home.

In 1811, they made the long 150-mile trek over the Cumberland Mountain plateau and took up residence at an attractive spot near the headquarters of Mulberry Creek, a branch of the Elk River at Maury County in Middle Tennessee.

Davy and Polly then moved to territory straddling Franklin County and Lincoln County, Tennessee, near the Alabama line, to eventually set up a home at Bean's Creek, near the present-day town of Winchester, which they called "Kentuck".

There, on the Mulberry fork of the Elk River tributary of the mighty Tennessee River, Davy marked his initials on a beach tree and laid out a five-acre claim on state land, and built a cabin home. This was great hunting country and Davy was able to indulge his passion as never before.

Unfortunately, the many home moves and the natural hardship Polly faced during cold and wet winters on the frontier sapped her energy and strength and, several months after giving birth to daughter Margaret, she died a very young woman in her late twenties, leaving David to care for three very small children.

Before Polly's death, Davy had been soldiering as a "mounted gunman" in the American army, battling with the Creek Indians at Fort Strother and Fort Taladega and encountering British troops in the Florida campaign. It was on leave for the birth of the third child that he found her in sickly condition.

No definite cause of death was established and historians say it may have been either typhoid or cholera. The illness, in the summer of 1815, lasted several weeks and when she died, a distraught Davy buried her on a hill near the cabin at Bean's Creek in Franklin County, Tennessee.

The gravestone, erected by the Tennessee Historical Commission, remembers Polly thus: "Polly Finlay Crockett. Born 1788 in Hamblen County. Married to David Crockett August 12, 1806. Mother of John Wesley Crockett—1807. William Crockett—1809. Margaret Finlay Crockett—1812. Died 1815."

Polly Finlay was very close to Davy Crockett's heart and it was said by associates that he "ever after" held the memory of his "tender and loving wife."

Within a year, however, David Crockett married again, to a widow Elizabeth Patton, mother of two children whose husband had been killed in the Creek War of 1812. Elizabeth, like Davy and Polly Finlay, was also of a Scots-Irish background.

Elizabeth was of a good family from North Carolina and owned a sizeable farm which helped Davy increase his social status in the frontier community.

But although he had taken on another wife and two more children, Davy's wandering lust and love of the wild frontier persisted, coupled with a blossoming political career which made him not just a Tennessee celebrity, but a great national hero in Washington.

In 1854, 18 years after Davy's violent death at The Alamo in Texas in March, 1836, Elizabeth Patton Crockett moved to the Lone Star state on land which was allocated to the family in lieu of Davy's heroic services at The Alamo and she died there in 1860, aged 72.

References:

Davis, William C. *Three Roads To the Alamo.* New York: HarperCollins Publishers, 1998.

Harper, Herbert L., ed. *Houston and Crockett : Heroes of Tennessee and Texas: an Anthology*. Nashville: Tennessee Historical Commission, 1986.

Lotaro, Michael A., ed. *Davy Crockett: The Man, The Legend, The Legacy*. Knoxville: University of Tennessee Press, 1985.

Van West, Carroll. *Tennessee Encyclopedia of History and Culture.* Tennessee Historical Society, 1998.

* Davy Crockett is remembered at his Limestone cabin birthplace at Greene County in East Tennessee alongside the Big Limestone and Nolichuckey Rivers thus: "Pioneer, Patriot, Soldier, Explorer, State Legislator, Congressman. Martyred at The Alamo. 1786-1836."

3

Selecting a Frontier Bride

AMERICAN FRONTIER FOLKLORE had some interesting tips for men on how to pick a wife:

- *Women with small ears are stingy and whining.*
- *If her hands feel cold, she is in love.*
- *If her thumbs stick out, she will be a hen-picker.*
- *If her second toe is longer than her big toe, she will be the boss of her husband.*

Women not wanting to become an old maid had to avoid:

- *Riding a mule.*
- *Stepping over a broom.*
- *Sitting on the table.*
- *Taking the last biscuit from the plate.*
- *Cutting their fingernails on a Sunday.*
- *Spilling salt.*
- *Cutting off the right angle of a piece of pie first.*

Some of the proverbial sayings from folk on the American frontier indicated a strong sense of inevitability in surroundings that for most of a century remained insecure:

- *Never trouble trouble, until trouble troubles you.*
- *Do not argue with the wind.*

- *If you sweep under a person' s feet, he (she) will never marry.*
- *To enter one door and exit another is bad luck.*
- *An axe under the bed will cure labour pains*
- *Kiss a red-haired person to cure fever blisters*
- *Today's today, and tomorrow's tomorrow.*
- *Come day, go day, God send Sunday.*
- *You can't rush God.*

Marry a man with an itching foot and a girl is bound to have anxieties. This was the common lot of the frontier woman. Better to go and share it with him.

Pork was a staple diet favoured by the Appalachian frontier women for their families. The women of the frontier maintained: "I hold a family to be in a desperate way when the mother can see the bottom of the pork barrel. For give me the children that's raised on good sound pork afore all the game in the country. Game's good as a relish and so's bread, but pork is the staff of life".

—From James Fenmore Cooper's *The Chainbearer*.

4

Eleanor Wilson

Patriot Woman Loyal to Her Family

ELEANOR WILSON was a woman of outstanding courage and singular mind who directly confronted the powerful British Army commander Lord Charles Cornwallis at her North Carolina home and firmly declared that her family was not going to desert the American patriot cause which they had espoused.

Robert Wilson, her husband, had emigrated with the family from Ulster with three brothers and other Presbyterian kinsmen, settling in the Carolinas in 1760 after spending a time in Pennsylvania.

One of the Wilson brothers, Zaccheus, was among the 27 signatories of the Mecklenburg Declaration on May 20, 1775, which staked for independence and was a documented marker for the ideals of the Scots-Irish settlers in the region.

Eleanor Wilson was in the vanguard of the patriot struggle and, with two of her sons, Robert and Joseph, taken prisoner at the surrender of Charleston, her resolve increased with the increase of hostilities in the war.

In another incident, Robert Wilson and son John were also captured while attempting to deliver provisions to the patriot lines. Among the prisoners held with them at the Camden, South Carolina jail was a teenage Andrew Jackson, along with some of his comrades from the nearby Waxhaw community.

Lord Cornwallis and his ruthless officer Banastra Tarleton, meanwhile, had decided to move on Charlotte, the main centre of rebellious unrest against the British, intent on forcing their will on the predominant Scots-Irish settlement.

It was to be a bloody conflict and reports of house burnings and plunderings in that 1780 expedition have merged into historical folklore in the Carolinas.

News that General Patrick Ferguson's Redcoat regiment had been routed at the Battle of Kings Mountain on October 7, 1780 riled Cornwallis and, it was while engaged in a realignment of his forces that the British commander halted for the night at Robert Wilson's Plantation near Steel Creek.

Lord Cornwallis, with his staff and Banastra Tarleton, occupied the Wilson home and he insisted on receiving provisions from Mrs Wilson. The conversation eventually came around to the committed Wilson family involvement as patriots in the Revolutionary War and Cornwallis tried unsuccessfully to enlist Eleanor Wilson to his cause.

Reportedly, he said: "Madam, your husband and your son are my prisoners; the fortune of war may soon place others of your sons, perhaps all of your kinsmen, in my power. Your sons are young, aspiring and brave. In a good cause, fighting for a generous King, such as George III, they might hope for rank, honor and wealth.

"If you could but induce your husband and sons to leave the rebels, and take up arms for a lawful sovereign I would almost pledge myself that they shall have rank and consideration in the British Army. If you, madam will pledge yourself to induce them to do so, I will immediately order their discharge."

In reply, Eleanor Wilson said her husband and children were very dear to her, but she insisted that she had felt, as a woman must, the trials and troubles which the War had brought. She was proud of her sons and in the struggle for liberty which they had engaged in.

"I have seven sons who are now, or have been, bearing arms. Indeed, my seventh son Zaccheus, who is only 15, has gone to take up the fight. Now sooner rather than see one of my family turn back from the glorious enterprise, I would myself enlist and show my husband and sons how to fight, and, if necessary, to die for their country."

Cornwallis was not amused and Banastra Tarleton interjected, "General, I think you've got into a Hornet's Nest"—ominously warning that he would see to it that Robert Wilson would never return home.

On the next day, young Zaccheus Wilson was captured by Redcoat scouts and handed over to Lord Cornwallis to act as his guide to the Catawba River.

At the River, Cornwallis was advised by the boy on the best ford to cross and in the crossing the soldiers found themselves in deep water, drawn in by a rapid current.

Zaccheus was hauled before an angry Cornwallis, who drew his sword and threatened to cut off the boy's head.

A cool Zaccheus, however, countered: "Don't you think it would be a cowardly act for you to strike an unarmed boy with your sword."

The General, taken by the boy's courage, stepped back and when his troops had successfully encountered the Catawba River he dismissed Zaccheus Wilson, telling him to return home to his mother.

References:

Ellet, Elizabeth F. *The Women of the American Revolution*. New York: Haskell House Publications, 1850 and 1969.

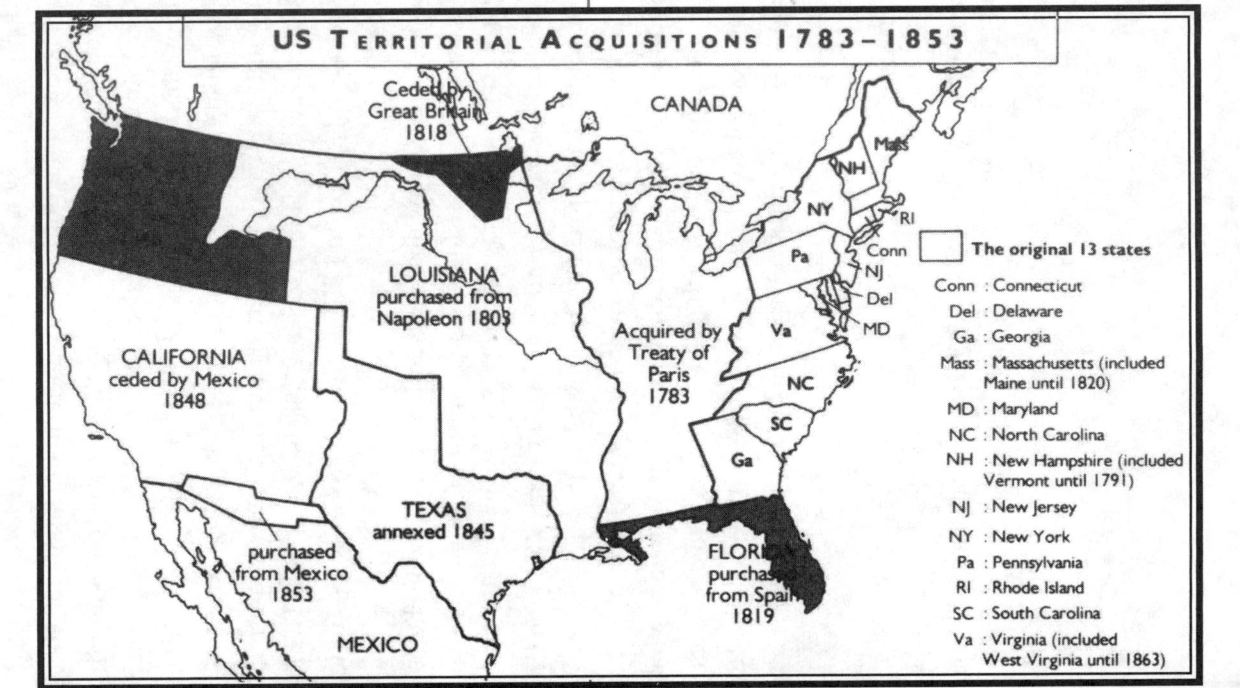
US TERRITORIAL ACQUISITIONS 1783–1853
Ceded by
Great Britain
1818
CANADA
LOUISIANA
purchased from
Napoleon 1803
Acquired by
Treaty of
Paris
1783
CALIFORNIA
ceded by Mexico
1848
TEXAS
annexed 1845
purchased
from Mexico
1853
MEXICO
from
1819
Mass
NH
NY
RI
Conn
Pa
NJ
Del
MD
Va
NC
SC
Ga
The original 13 states
Conn : Connecticut
Del : Delaware
Ga : Georgia
Mass : Massachusetts (included Maine until 1820)
MD : Maryland
NC : North Carolina
NH : New Hampshire (included Vermont until 1791)
NJ : New Jersey
NY : New York
Pa : Pennsylvania
RI : Rhode Island
SC : South Carolina
Va : Virginia (included West Virginia until 1863)

5

Mary Johnston
Community Leader in a War Zone

MARY JOHNSTON was a South Carolina heroine who in 1769 emigrated as an eight-year-old with her parents Matthew and Jane Gaston Johnston. The Presbyterian family had come from Ballymoney, Co Antrim in the north of Ireland and they landed at Charleston, eventually moving up to Chester County in the Piedmont area.

The Johnstons later became embroiled in the Revolutionary War and as a militiaman Matthew saw battle against the Cherokee Indians in 1776 along with a nephew James, who was to marry his daughter in 1780.

In the middle of the War these cousins had little time for the pursuits of marriage and very early in the hostilities Mary received the shocking news of her husband's injury and her father's death.

James Johnston was promoted to captain in the State troops and he commanded a company at the Battle of Kings Mountain in October, 1780 and continued in army uniform until the end of the War.

In his absence, Mary Johnston, who was aged only about twenty,, combined the role of farmer on the family settlement at Fishing Creek, with that of a very active community leader of the women in the region, effectively operating as the eyes and ears of the patriot movement.

The close surveillance in the region courageously mounted by Mary Johnston and other gutsy females from these Scots-Irish communities allowed the militia men (their husbands, brothers, sons and nephews) to breach the dangers for occasional trips home.

Mary Johnston, the mother of seven children, was awarded an army pension when James died in 1797 and her significant contribution to the patriot cause in the War was also recognised.

References:

Ellet, Elizabeth F. *The Women of the American Revolution*. New York: Haskell House Publications, 1850 and 1969.

6

Sarah Robinson Erwin

FACING DOWN INVADERS

THIS WIFE of an American patriot soldier at the battles of Kings Mountain and Cowpens bravely resisted a British army attack on her Carolina home while her husband was at the front line.

Sarah Robinson Erwin, the mother of six children, gave shelter in the family home to a badly wounded patriot soldier, Samuel Alexander, and when a Redcoat detachment arrived to seize him, Sarah bluntly refused entry.

As she stood in the doorway of the log cabin home blocking entry, a soldier violently struck Sarah on the forehead with his sabre and opened a deep cut. But bleeding profusely, she still continued to strongly resist the intruders, who, shocked by her reactions, withdrew from the area.

Samuel Alexander recovered from his wounds, but Sarah did not and, after suffering continually from her injuries, she died within a few years, aged only 34. Her resistance had resulted in her death.

Sarah was a daughter of James and Catherine Robinson, of Lancaster County, South Carolina, a Scots-Irish family which settled early in the Carolinas.

Her husband Colonel Alexander Erwin, of Burke County, North Carolina, commanded a company of mounted (militia) infantry and his older brother Arthur also fought with the patriots at Kings Mountain.

The Erwins were an Ulster Presbyterian family, with Nathaniel and his wife Leah emigrating to Philadelphia in 1740 before moving to York County, South Carolina. Arthur was born in the north of Ireland about 1738, and Alexander in Pennsylvania in 1750. Alexander, when he quit soldiering, was a court clerk and a North Carolina state legislator.

Sarah Robinson Erwin is buried beside her husband at Quaker Meadow's Presbyterian cemetery in North Carolina.

References:

Craig, Erwin, Johnston, Davis and Owen Genealogy, 1988.

Paris, Captain R. L., Calhoun: Georgia.

7

Rachel (Donelson) Jackson

FRONTIER WOMAN AND PRESIDENT'S WIFE

THE EXTREME harshness of the American frontier during the late 18th century made life very difficult for women young and old as they struggled to keep pace with the enormous challenges encountered by their men-folk in what was a wooded and mountainous wilderness.

Rachel Donelson, who later became the wife of the seventh United States President Andrew Jackson, was only twelve when she and members of her family and Scots-Irish associates embarked on one of the most daunting and perilous journeys in America's early history.

For a girl as young, intelligent and lively as the dark-haired Rachel, the arduous and highly dangerous Holston River voyage to the Cumberland River in Middle Tennessee region obviously left a lasting impression and the harrowing experience was indeed character-building for the numerous personal trials she was to face later in her life.

Rachel (Donelson) Jackson was born in 1767 in Pittsylvania County, Virginia after her parents had moved there from the eastern side of the state where they were married.

John Donelson, Rachel's father, was a land-owner and huntsman/ surveyor in Virginia and North Carolina who became a leader of the Watauga community which settled during the 1770s on the Holston River of what today is North East Tennessee.

The Wataugans, led by another Scots-Irishman James Robertson, were a hardy, tough breed of people who had the insatiable urge to keep pushing the frontier westwards to new settlements, across the Allegheny Mountains—even against the advice of British land agents who feared the inevitable conflict with the native American tribes. In that region, the Indian tribes were the Cherokees and the Chickasaws.

John Donelson and James Robertson combined with a North Carolina lawyer and agent Richard Henderson to make an assault on new lands on the Cumberland River several hundred miles west. The plans were first prepared in 1777 and Robertson led an exploratory team there over a two-year period, before the decision was taken to move.

A 3,000-acre land grant was negotiated with Richard Henderson and arrangements were made for the movement of these families who were prepared to risk all to start a new life in a far-distant rugged wilderness.

The journey was split with James Robertson assigned to led 200 men and boys with their animals (horses, cows, pigs and sheep) and other belongings on the Kentucky route, along the Wilderness Road and through the Cumberland Gap.

John Donelson, with the welfare of his wife Rachel and young daughter Rachel and his nine other children uppermost in his thoughts, led, with male comrades, the 400 women and children on a flotilla of flat boats from Fort Patrick Henry along the Holston River to the Cumberland River and the new settlement of Fort Nashborough, later to be named Nashville.

River travel, because of the obvious dangers of attack from Indians, was not a favoured mode of communication in that part of the Appalachian frontier, but the Wataugan people felt there was no other option.

It was an extremely cold winter—said to be coldest in living memory in North Carolina and the Tennessee territory with the deep snow and frozen rivers making the journey for both parties extremely hazardous, but with dogged determination they persevered and by Christmas week of 1779 Robertson and his men had arrived at their destination.

They were worn out by the rigours of the journey, but began almost immediately to erect log cabins and clear stretches of land for the arrival of John Donelson and the families in the spring. The Cumberland River was frozen over and the animal stock had to be driven across rock solid ice.

The Donelson-piloted party moved in an armada of 40 small flat boats and canoes, moving slowly along the Holston River. The largest boat, Adventure, had 30 families on board, including James Robertson's wife Charlotte and five children and John Donelson's own family, his wife Rachel and the children including young Rachel.

It was a journey into the unknown for the families; along unchartered waters, over dangerous shoals, rapids and falls; through territory occupied by hostile Indian tribes and in weather conditions well below zero temperatures.

After only three miles the voyage was halted; ice and snow and cold had set in and the frozen river made progress impossible. There was no movement until mid-February, and when the boats were eventually cut loose, they were hampered again by the swell of the river due to incessant heavy rain.

Several boats sank and some of the voyagers took ill from smallpox and died. As they passed the Chickamauga Indian settlements the boats came under attack from tribesmen massed on the shore. There were casualties on both sides, with settlers countering the Indian assaults with sniper fire from their long Kentucky rifles.

Most of the boats got through, beyond the danger points, and by the beginning of spring they were at the mouth of the Tennessee River and the high water of the Ohio River. They faced difficult upstream currents and progress was further hampered, when they had to stop and make camp to replenish dwindling food supplies by hunting buffalo and bear in the adjoining woods.

The last lap of the journey came via the Cumberland River and on Monday April 24 when the party reached French Salt Lick, site of present-day down-town Nashville, there was a hearty welcome from James Robertson and his men who had prepared well for the arrival.

When they reached Fort Nashborough in 1780, John Donelson settled his family on fertile bottom land, a few miles from the fort, but this was dangerous territory and with a scarcity of grain and food for the winter, they moved to a more settled area at Harrodsburg, Kentucky in the fall (autumn) of that year.

In 1785, Rachel, in her 18th year, married Lewis Robards, who was from a good family in Mercer County, Kentucky. But it was a relationship which lasted only a few years and Rachel returned to be with her mother, who had moved back to live near Nashville after the murder of her husband in 1786 by persons unknown on the road between Nashville and Kentucky.

The death of John Donelson was a severe blow to his family and it was at her mother's home that Rachel met a young lawyer from North Carolina, Andrew Jackson, who was staying as a boarding guest.

The friendship developed and in August, 1791 the pair were married at Natchez, but the marriage to Lewis Robards was never officially wound up which meant Rachel had unwittingly committed bigamy when she wed Andrew Jackson.

Robards had filed divorce proceedings to the Virginia legislature, but dropped these without telling Rachel and it was an inconclusive arrangement that was to haunt Mrs Jackson in later years.

By September 1793, Robards did manage to get his divorce, after charging that it was his wife who had deserted him and was living an "adulterous relationship" with another man. The charge was not contested, and Rachel and Andrew went through another marriage ceremony, quietly in Nashville in January, 1794.

Rachel came with a settlement of her late father's estate, which included household articles valued $433.33 and two black slaves. The

Rachel Jackson, painting by R.E.W. Earl (1827)
From The Hermitage: Home of President Andrew Jackson

couple had no children, but they had a very happy 37-year marriage, even though the last few years were marred by allegations made by political opponents of Andrew over the legality of their marriage after Rachel's break-up with Lewis Robards.

During the early years of the marriage, Andrew Jackson was a lawyer, circuit judge, land speculator, farmer and businessman. He later moved into politics, was a soldier of national renown especially for his victory over the British at the Battle of New Orleans in 1815 and, eventually, he became President, serving two terms in Washington from 1828 to 1836.

From a life as a child and teenager in the harsh Tennessee and Kentucky frontier wilderness, Rachel's personal circumstances improved immeasurably and in the several large plantation homes where they lived, her role was more supervisory of the housekeeping and manual duties which were carried out by the black slaves.

She hosted regular gatherings for members of the large family circle and Jackson's political and business friends, but she fretted much over her husband's long absences from home, due to his exploits as a soldier and politician.

In 1808, they adopted one of twin sons born to her sister-in-law Elizabeth Donelson and eventually Andrew Jackson Jr. was made President Jackson's heir.

Tragically, Rachel Jackson died a few weeks after Andrew was elected for his first four-year term as President. It came soon after the death of another adopted child, 16-year-old Indian son Lyncoya. Devastated, Rachel's condition rapidly deteriorated on learning of the vicious accusations of "bigamy and adultery", made against her during the Presidential campaign of 1828.

Rachel was heartbroken that she should be targeted in this way and, within a few weeks, her physical and mental condition had considerably worsened. Although Andrew tried frantically to revive her, she died on December 22, 1828.

She was buried in the garden of their Hermitage home outside Nashville on Christmas Eve. Among the pall-bearers at the funeral was Sam Houston, then Governor of Tennessee and a close associate of Jackson.

The Hermitage, home of Rachel and Andrew Jackson

For several days, the incoming President was inconsolable and he told his aides that "a loss so great can be compensated by no earthly gift." He had to prepare for the trip to Washington, to begin his Presidency, but until the day he died in 1845, Andrew grieved for a wife who was so close and dear to him.

Andrew's love for his wife, over thirty seven years of marriage, was evident by the inscription he placed on Rachel's tomb.

It was said he kept his pistols polished and in condition for instant use against anyone who cast a shadow of discredit or doubt on the honour of the woman he loved with "such single-minded, fierce and gentle devotion".

The inscription on Rachel's tombstone read: "Here lies the remains of Mrs Rachel Jackson, wife of President Jackson, who died 22nd December, 1828, aged 61. Her face was fair; her person pleasing, her temper amiable and her heart kind.

"She delighted in relieving the wants of her fellow creatures and cultivated that divine pleasure by the most liberal and unpretending methods; to the poor she was a benefactor; to the rich an example; to the wretched a comforter; to the prosperous an ornament; her piety went hand in hand with her benevolence, and she thanked her creator for being permitted to do good.

"A being so gentle and yet so virtuous, slander might wound, but not dishonor. Even death when he bore her from the arms of her husband, could but transport her to the bosom of her God."

References:

Booraem, Hendrik. *Young Hickory: The Making of Andrew Jackson.* Dallas, Texas: Taylor Publishing Company, 2001.

Cruse, Katherine W. *An Amiable Woman: Rachel Jackson*. Nashville: The Ladies' Hermitage Association, 1994.

Degregorio, William A. *The Complete Book of US Presidents.* Avenel, New Jersey: Random House Publishing, 1984.

Dykeman, Wilma. *Tennessee: A New History.* Newport, Tennessee: Wakestone Books, 1984.

Kunhardt Jr., Philip B., Philip B. Kunhardt III and Peter W. Kunhardt. *The American President.* New York: Riverhead Books, 1999.

McPherson, James M., ed. *To the Best of My Ability: The American Presidents.* New York: Dorling Kindersley Books, 2000.

Nashville: The Hermitage Historical Collection.

Remini, Robert V. *The Life of Andrew Jackson.* New York: Penguin Books, 1988.

Van West, Carroll, ed. *Tennessee Encyclopedia of History and Culture*. Nashville: Tennessee Historical Society, 1998.

8

Sterling Valour of the Women of Tennessee

IN THE ANNALS of all countries there is no age nor face that has given more sterling valor than that displayed by the frontier woman of Tennessee. She shared with the men all the dangers of the wilderness with its toils. She came with the first settlers and bore with fortitude the privations of a forest cabin.

"No other border life of recent times, in our territories, presents such a wonderful growth and change from wild backwoods to the dignity of a state in 26 years.

"To her presence more than any one influence, to her moral worth and example, is due the high rank attained and the end achieved in so short a time. She did not wait for the clearing and the building of the cabin and the planting of the crops—she went along and helped to do these things.

"She rocked the cradle in the home—swung the cradle in the field. She spun the flax and carded the wool and made the clothing for the family. She has gone to the aid of the sick neighbour and returned to find her own home in ashes.

"When rumours of Indian raids reached the settlements she went to the fort prepared to do a man's part should the exigency of the hour demand.

"In such a test of courage, she stood, gun in hand, beside the dead body of a man who had fallen, the victim of a besieger's bullet. And still the mother's thoughtful care over her children never left her. She trained them at her knee. The frontier woman of Tennessee never lacked for courage nor opportunities to prove it.

"There was a peculiar trait which seemed to be born in the children of that day, or which mothers had taught them—to make no show or fear nor make alarm, much like the young birds, which, at a call, seek the cover of a wing. It was a hush of caution, rather than of fear."

References:

Taylor, Oliver. *Historic Sullivan: Tennessee.* Johnson City, Tennessee: Overmountain Press, 1988.

9

Nancy (Anderson) Green

STEELY WIDOW OF THE FRONTIER

THIS FORMIDABLE Scots-Irish woman of the Carolina back country was born in Ballymoney, Co Antrim in the north of Ireland about 1750, of devout Presbyterian Covenanting stock, and the fascinating story of her life on the American frontier is one of tragedy, deprivation and ultimate happiness.

Nancy and her Stinson (Stephenson) family (who included brothers James and William) moved to America in 1772 under the pastoral care of radical Presbyterian minister, Rev William Martin, and settled at Rocky Creek, a branch of the Catawba River in Chester County, South Carolina.

Just before she left her homeland, Nancy married a Co Antrim kinsman William Anderson and on arrival in South Carolina they were allocated a track of land given as bounty by the colonial authorities as inducement to emigration from Europe.

By 1773, William Anderson had built a log cabin and set about planting some Indian corn to complement the foods that he would readily find by fishing in the rivers and hunting in the forests.

Gradually, the Anderson homestead advanced in size and with three young children (Mary, Robert and William) to feed and clothe

William and Nancy had to work long hours to ensure they had a reasonable level of return from what then was effectively an outer frontier region.

The Revolutionary War, which had started, heightened tensions in the area and even at church worship on a Sunday the settlers were confronted with the stark choice on how they should react—either succumbing to the rule of the Crown forces or throwing in their lot with the American patriot cause.

For the Rev William Martin, an old-style Presbyterian pastor with strong views on independence for his people and a deep distrust of the British, there was only one option.

"My hearers," William Martin said in his broad Ulster accent to faithful worshippers like William and Nancy Anderson, "Talk and angry words will not do. We must fight."

After hearing the Rev William Martin, William Anderson felt he had a patriotic duty to fulfil—to join the local militia and take up the fight.

His wife Nancy fully understood the predicament, but as William bade her and the children farewell at the cabin door before heading off on horseback to join the local unit, she might not have imagined that it would be the last time they would see each other.

A bout of smallpox was visited on Nancy and the family and, with William away, British dragoons stopped off to maliciously plunder on the homestead and drive off the stock in the fields.

Other cabins belonging to Scots-Irish settlers were raided in similar fashion and the nearby Presbyterian meeting house where the Rev William Martin was pastor was burnt down as a reprisal against the patriot militiamen and their supporters.

Nancy was in a hopeless position and for food she had to roast the ears of green corn, or dry the corn in milk and grate it on a rough stone into coarse meal, from which she made mush for herself and her sick children.

William Anderson, meanwhile, joined the forces of General Thomas Sumter under Captain John Steel at Clem's Branch on the east side of the Catawba River, and he fought at the battles of Williamsons, Rocky Mount, Hanging Rock and Carey's Fort.

But two months after he left William was shot dead in a Redcoat attack on his unit. Nancy was now a widow, left alone to look after three young children. Indeed, in the small Rocky Creek neighbourhood four other women were widowed by the deaths of their husbands in battle.

Eventually, the smallpox epidemic cleared and the children recovered, but the onerous tasks of harvesting and attending to the daily painstaking chores of the home kept Nancy and the other widows fully occupied.

The stock had gone, but Nancy Anderson pulled her flax, watered and put it through the break before scuttling it with the hand-scuttle and hackling it on the coarse and fine hackle. She then carefully spun the flax in a manner she had been taught back in her north of Ireland homeland.

Nancy did receive some help from her brother William Stinson, who was engaged at the Battle of Kings Mountain and paid regular visits to Rocky Creek. He had to be very careful as British and loyalist forces were constantly passing through the area, and regularly harassed Nancy Anderson and the other women.

The food which Nancy Anderson and her children lived on over that winter was mainly bread, although occasionally a little meat was given to her by patrolling patriots, after hunting in the forests.

Nancy had to be adaptable and she learned to fish in the adjoining river and steams, using traps, and the catches she got did provide a staple and a very welcome change of diet.

Throughout her ordeal, Nancy Anderson never wavered from her strong Covenanting faith and she constantly prayed for a betterment of the situation.

This was to come in a rather unusual way in the form of a stranger Daniel Green, thought to be a soldier, who accidentally came upon the Anderson homestead at Rocky Creek.

The tall, quite apprehensive Green introduced himself to Mrs Anderson and her children and after giving her some firm assurances about his reasons for being in the area, he was invited to partake of a meal.

Nancy and the stranger talked for hours about the extremely difficult personal plight both found themselves in and while he said he needed to borrow a horse, there was a marked reluctance to take the lone sorrel mare which the poor widow Anderson had.

Several days elapsed and the friendship between Nancy Anderson and the stranger developed into a mutual relationship which grew stronger as time passed. Even a week on the bleak landscape of the American frontier was a lengthy period for a vulnerable widow and a soldier uncertain about his future. Nancy and Daniel had only known each other five days.

Obviously there was no time to hang around and, after borrowing a horse, the stranger rode with Nancy Anderson to the home of the local Justice John Gaston, where, after a short legal ceremony, the pair were pronounced man and wife. A dollar payment was passed over – all the money Daniel Green possessed in the world.

Mrs Anderson became Mrs Green in a lightning marriage which led to raised eyebrows among the strict very conservative Presbyterian Covenanting community of Rocky Creek. Acquaintances were scandalised that Nancy had dispensed with the marital formalities laid down by the church.

In Presbyterian Covenanting tradition an intended marriage had to be published by the minister on three successive Sundays. This Nancy and Daniel Green did not do. Nancy, however, was undeterred by the criticism. It was her judgment and personal choice that Daniel Green was a loving partner, and a suitable, caring step-father for her three young children.

Daniel was a man of commanding stature, said to be frank and honourable in his dealings, aptly disposed to trust and possessing a sound intellect. Nancy had learned that Daniel was born of a poor family background in New Jersey about 1752 which made them around the same age.

During the early part of the Revolutionary War he had served in Canada and moving to Philadelphia, about 30 miles from his home, he had a spell in the marines.

He returned to military service as a patriot soldier and was captured by the British and held on a prison ship at Charleston, before escaping along with a number of Scots-Irish lads from Chester, York and Lancaster counties of South Carolina.

Daniel and Nancy Green eventually overcame their adversities caused by the War, and the murmurings within the Rocky Creek community about the standing of their hurried marriage within church confines. Their prosperity increased, but they had no children and Daniel lovingly treated Nancy's daughter and two sons as his own.

Daniel joined Nancy as a committed churchgoer and he repaired the Presbyterian church at Beckhamville, which was damaged in the War, and built an ornate granite wall around the burial ground. Daniel did not belong to any particular denomination, unlike his wife, but he was highly esteemed by members of different faiths as an excellent man, a sincere Christian.

Nancy lived until she was 77, passing away in June 1827 after a lengthy illness. Daniel, on the day of her funeral, remarked that they had been together for 50 years and had tasted real happiness.

"We have been blessed in our basket and our store, flourishing like a green bay tree beside the waters, but this is not our abiding place. How soon I too may go the way of all living, I know not," he said.

Daniel survived Nancy by only a few weeks. He was a man in his late seventies and had grown very tired nursing and watching his ailing wife in her final days. A severe attack of fever led to his death.

Funeral arrangements for Daniel were made by his step-son William Anderson, a highly respected colonel in the American militia. Just before Nancy's death, William had gone to the spot where his father William had been buried and removed the remains to where he expected soon to open a grave for his mother.

Heavy rains had resulted in the original burying ground being flooded, with the bones of people buried there being brought to the surface.

It was a harrowing experience and extremely distressful to Nancy Anderson Green when she was told. But due to her very poor state of health, she was unable to be present at the transfer with other family members.

In a quiet reserved spot near the banks of the Catawba River which flows through the beautiful countryside which straddles South Carolina and North Carolina, Nancy Anderson was buried between her two soldier husbands, alongside her children, grandchildren and great-grandchildren.

Nancy was most certainly a woman of extraordinary character and courage, typical of those who settled in the 18th century American frontier, and against great odds made a settled home and reared a family.

Maritime records show that James Stinson, Nancy's brother, emigrated from Larne in Co Antrim to Charleston in South Carolina on August 25, 1772 on the James and Mary sailing ship.

The James and Mary was one of five vessels which that year carried 467 families (more than 1,000 people) of Covenanting (Reformed Presbyterian) stock from Co Antrim to America on an historic passage arranged and led by the Rev William Martin.

James Stinson was a militia captain under Colonel John Sevier at the Battle of Kings Mountain in October 7, 1780 and his brother William also fought there.

William Stinson is listed on a memorial to 65 Revolutionary War soldiers from the Rev William Martin's Catholic Presbyterian Church at Chester County, South Carolina. Most of the soldiers were either north of Ireland born or first or second generation Ulster-Scots.

References:

Ellet, Elizabeth F. *The Women of the American Revolution*. New York: Haskell House Publishers, 1969.

Moss, Bobby Gilmer. *The Patriots of Kings Mountain*. Blacksburg, South Carolina: Scotia-Hibernia Press, 1990.

10

Margaret "Peggy" Brown

An Evergreen Frontier Matriarch

FRONTIER WOMEN did not come any tougher and hardier than Margaret 'Peggy' Brown, who was born in Co Antrim in the north of Ireland in April 1701 and died in Middle Tennessee in September 1801, aged one hundred years, five months and 17 days.

Margaret was a real American pioneer, a matriarch, who, when she was 84, braved the perils of the frontier with her family and in-laws in a journey of hundreds of miles over mountains, through forests and across dangerous Indian country from North Carolina to a new settlement on the Cumberland River in Middle Tennessee.

The journey was to have very tragic results for the wider Brown family.

Family records show that Peggy Brown's father, Joseph Fleming, was a land owner of substance in Ulster and as a teenager she married William Brown, a farmer from Londonderry, where the couple lived for a number of years and where six of their seven children (four sons and three daughters) were born.

Members of the Brown and Fleming families defended the walled city of Londonderry in Ulster for the Protestant Williamite cause during the famous Siege there in 1688-89.

William and Peggy Brown sailed for America in 1745, landing at New Castle, Delaware, settling over a period at Lancaster County, Pennsylvania and the Shenandoah Valley in Virginia.

The Browns moved to North Buffalo Creek in Guilford County, North Carolina to take up a land grant of 411 acres from the Earl of Granville, acting on behalf of King George II, but William did not live long to enjoy the newly-acquired land and he died in December, 1757, aged 70.

His wife Peggy was 14 years younger and, with the family gathered around her, she doggedly maintained the frontier farm land, instilling a determination within the family circle to resist any danger that came their way from hostile Indian attack.

Colonel James Brown, a son, moved with his wife Jane Gillespie after the Revolutionary War from Guilford County in North Carolina to Maury County in Middle Tennessee. He had been given a certificate payable in western lands for his military service and the move had tragic consequences for the family in May 1788.

James made a preliminary trip to the region to select a track of land and, while he returned to round up the family for the journey to new territory, two sons Daniel and William were left to prepare a clearing and build a log cabin.

A large boat was built on the Holston River and two-inch planks placed around the gunwales had holes for firing and the vessel was equipped with a small swivel gun to ward off hostile Indians on the dangerous river journey along the Tennessee River to Middle Tennessee.

The party that set off included James Brown, his wife Jane (Gillespie), four sons James, John, Joseph and George; three daughters Jane, Elizabeth and Polly, five other young men and a black women

Five days after leaving the Holston River region, the Browns were "befriended" at the Tennessee River just west of present-day Chattanooga by Indian chief Cotetoy and two of his tribesmen from the Tuskagee River reservation.

Other Indians were alerted and 40 of them arrived in a fleet of canoes, hoisting a flag of truce. They said they wanted to trade, but hidden under their blankets were rifles. Unwittingly, James Brown allowed them to board the boat, with tragic results.

In a bloody assault James Brown's head was cut from his body and thrown into the river. Two of his sons, James and John, as well as the five young men who had joined the family were also killed in the massacre. The surviving members—wife Jane, and five children—were taken captive.

One son was detained by the Shawnee tribe for five years and Jane Brown and one of her daughters were forced to march hundreds of miles to Ohio. They returned to settle at the Duck River in Maury County and the county's first court was held in the log cabin home of a son Joseph, one of those held captive by the Indians.

Jane Gillespie Brown, whose Gillespie family had emigrated from Ulster at about the same time as the Browns, lived at Maury County until her death in 1831. She was 48 when the massacre occurred.

In September 1794, the Brown sons Daniel, William, Joseph and George obtained revenge for the massacre of their brothers when they wiped out the Indian settlement at Nickajack.

Before they left on this expedition, Jane Brown said: "The Brown women will wait while their men folk ride off. We've waited before, and we can wait again. It is the lot of women to wait. We'll be here when you come home."

On Jane Brown's tombstone in a disused cemetery off the Main Street in Columbia, the county capital, is an inscription relating the facts of the May, 1788 massacre and carrying a tragic footnote: "The reason I tell you these things O reader is so that you will know at what cost this liberty which you enjoy today was won for you. People lost their lives and liberty in obtaining this good land that you enjoy."

A few months before the Brown attack three frontier surveyors Captain William Pruett, Moses Brown and Daniel Johnston were killed by Indians and, in another incident, leading frontiersman Anthony Bledsoe lost his life.

These attacks were avenged by the local militia force, led by James Robertson, one of the heroes of the Battle of Kings Mountain and a leader of the Watauga settlement in East Tennessee.

The Brown massacre and other Indian killings had a devastating effect on the Scots-Irish settler families in the region and tensions remained high for several decades until peace treaties and population movement of the tribes brought the violent hostilities to an end.

Peggy Brown, the family matriarch, spent her later days with her youngest daughter Jane, who married Reese Porter, son of an Ulster-born couple, Hugh and Violet Mackey Porter. Peggy is buried at Springhill Cemetery near Nashville.

Hugh Porter was a justice of the peace at Orange County, North Carolina and he owned 293 acres of land close to the Brown homesteads in Guilford County. Reese served with his father in the militia and in the Revolutionary War he was at the Battle of Guilford Courthouse.

Family records claim Jane Porter stole through enemy lines during the War to free her husband, who was being held captive in a log cabin, and for his military service, Reese received land grants of 3,640 acres at the Tennessee, Elk and Duck Rivers in Middle Tennessee.

The problem with this land was that Cherokee Indians still had the legal rights to it, and during the twenty years of a protracted wrangle Reese Porter and his family lived at Nashville (Fort Nashborough).

His wife Jane died just before they were given the go-ahead in 1806 to move on to the land and the family plantation on Reese's death extended to more than 2,500 acres.

Grandsons of William and Peggy Brown fought with General Andrew Jackson in the War of 1812: Lieutenant Colonel Joseph Brown, commanding the 27th Infantry Regiment and serving alongside his cousin Lieutenant William Porter.

The Browns and the Porters, who were also connected through marriage with the Pillow and Sterrett families from Ulster, were strong Presbyterian stock, closely identified with congregations in various American frontier regions where they settled.

References:

Harkness, David J. "Colonial Heroines of Tennessee, Kentucky and Virginia." Compiled by University of Tennessee, 1974.

Nashville: Tennessee State Library and Archives Museum.

Nashville: Tennessee Historical Society Collection.

David Wright

11

Sacagawea

Trusted Guide to a Great Exploration

THE CELEBRATED 1804-06 expedition from the Mississippi to the Pacific by explorers Captain Meriwether Lewis and Captain William Clark may not have been completed without the help of a young Shoshoni Indian woman from the Mandan tribal community known as Sacagawea.

The 16-year-old was married to a French-Canadian trapper Toussaint Charbonneau and they were both enlisted for the Lewis-Clark expedition, with Charbonneau as an interpreter of the Indian languages and Sacagawea as a direct influential link to the tribes.

During the journey from Missouri to Montana, Lewis and Clark encountered a Shoshoni chief, who turned out to the Sacagawea's brother and he sold them horses and gave valuable logistical help on the way ahead.

Sacagawea had given birth to a baby as the party was setting off in the first spring of the momentous journey, the concept of President Thomas Jefferson after he had purchased the extensive Louisiana lands to the west of the Mississippi River from the French government for fifteen million dollars.

Sacagawea carried her infant son through mountain trails and white-water streams in fragile canoes in the largely unchartered territory.

She spoke many Indian dialects and was able to communicate through sign language. As a woman she was a sign of peace to the tribes which the explorers and their party encountered.

This strong courageous native American woman interpreted for the two explorers, rescued their gear when a boat seized, and obtained horses for them from local Indians. She literally earned herself a legendary place in Indian folklore (her brother being a Shoshoni chief) as the woman who showed America the way west.

Incredibly, Sacagawea is merely recorded in the journals of Lewis and Clark as "the Indian woman" because they could not spell her name. But the contribution she made to the success of the long trek over the Rockies and on to the Pacific coastline was outstanding.

In 1806 Sacagawea and her husband were reunited with her Shoshoni tribe after they left the Lewis-Clark expedition.

Some accounts say Sacagawea died from a disease in 1812, while others say she lived to be an old woman, settling on the Wind River Reservation in Wyoming where she was buried.

Legend has it Sacagawea made a beaded belt from blue beads given to her by Lewis and Clark in appreciation of the help in guiding them on the epic journey to the far west of America.

The significance of the bluebelt is one of friendship and unselfish generosity; of how this courageous young woman gave one of her most prized possessions to acquire a magnificent sea otter robe that neither Clark and Lewis had managed to purchase from a Chinook Indian.

The fascinating story of the Blue Belt emerged from the Lewis-Clark "Corps of Discovery" in their remarkable expedition on behalf of President Jefferson and the American Government from Missouri to California in 1804-06.

The excellent Blue Belt painting is by artist David Wright, from Gallatin, Tennessee, and it is part of the Gray Stone Press (Nashville) collection.

We acknowledge the courtesy of David Wright and Gray Stone Press for permission to use this and other paintings in the book.

The Blue Belt by David Wright

(Sacagawea & Captain William Clark just east of the Great Falls)
From the collection of Norm & Toodie Burke

References:

Davis, William C. *The American frontier: Pioneers, Settlers and Cowboys 1800-1899*. University of Oklahoma Press, 1992.

Faragher, John Mack. *The American Heritage: Encyclopedia of American History*. New York: Henry Holt Incorporated, 1998.

The Wild West. Warner Books.

Thom, James Alexander. *From Sea to Shining Sea*. New York: Ballentine Books, 1984.

12

Mary Neely

EXTRAORDINARY WOMAN WHO DEFIED HER INDIAN CAPTIVES

THE SURVIVAL of young Mary Neely after being captured by Indians on the death of her father is an extraordinary story which aptly epitomises the determination and courage of settlers on the 18th century American frontier.

Mary was the fourth of a family of ten children, born to William and Margaret (Patterson) Neely near the French Broad River in North Carolina in 1761. The family was of Ulster and Welsh extraction, having emigrated a few years earlier.

William Neely was a restless adventurous man who set his sights on acquiring new land in the Tennessee territory, then belonging to North Carolina, and with six other pioneers he headed in the direction of the Cumberland River in mid-Tennessee by means of a large canoe which he had built from a large poplar tree.

After selling his possessions in North Carolina, William moved about 1779 with 96 cattle and 40 horses from the French Broad River to a point on the Cumberland River, about twelve miles east of present-day Nashville, which he settled and called Neely's Bend.

William's teenage daughter Mary travelled with him in the canoe on the perilous river journey through hostile Indian country, while the rest of the family arrived by land.

William Neely was obviously a leader in this frontier settlement, for his counsel was sought in every enterprise, especially when danger protruded from an Indian attack.

In the first year of the settlement William Neely and his people had to live on meat, vegetables and fruit, as their little stock of flour and meal had run out. It was while engaged in corn producing that an incident occurred which led to William's death and changed the whole course of Mary's life.

About 30 of the men from the settlement were at a spring, two and a half miles from the fort, making salt and clearing off ground for cultivation the next year. They appeared relaxed, as no sign of Indians had been noticed for quite some time.

Two hours before sunset, William told the men to return to the fort and he and Mary would stay there alone. Some of the men protested, fearful it was too dangerous to leave him and 19-year-old Mary so exposed, but William was a person without fear and he stayed behind with his daughter.

Indians, however, were lurking in the trees watching the operations and they pounced shortly after the men had gone, fatally wounding William with a tomahawk blow to the head. Mary stood helpless, shouting frantically to her father to reach for his gun.

She fainted with the shock of the attack and the mortal blow on her father and when she regained consciousness a few minutes later she realised two Indians were dragging her towards their canoe.

That fateful memory of those few minutes remained with Mary for the rest of her life and later when she returned to the white settlements she would describe it as the saddest day of her life.

But Mary was taken north of the Cumberland River to an Indian reservation in Kentucky and she was to spend the next few years in the custody of her captors.

Initially, Mary thought she would suffer the same fate as her father, but death did not materialise and after deliberations at an Indian council it was decided to offer her the choice of either becoming the wife of a young tribesman or a servant to the chief.

She chose the latter. The idea of becoming the wife of the one who may have murdered her father appalled Mary and, to her surprise, the decision she made was honoured.

For a month after her father died Mary could not shed a tear, and, continually watched by the Indians, she longed for her freedom. Even when she was being taken away from the Cumberland region to the reservation she managed to carve marks on trees to guide those who might pursue, or set a guide for her if she managed to escape.

A favourite past-time of the Indians in the evening was to get out the scalps they had taken and dry them in front of the fire. Mary, as she watched their barbarous actions, must have been horrified that perhaps her father's scalp was one of those being paraded in front of her.

As time passed the watch on Mary became more relaxed, and one night, while encamped under a beech tree she took the opportunity to escape. She climbed on to the branches of the tree and hid, but the Indians were alerted to her presence and she was promptly returned to her post.

In the first winter of her capture smallpox afflicted a large number in the reservation and Mary too was smitten, with sores appearing all over her body. During the epidemic the Indian meat supplies ran out, and they were all forced to drink bear oil, of which the tribes always seemed to carry a supply.

Revolted by its taste, Mary, however, did not partake of the oil and for days she starved, getting by only on pieces of white oak bark which she peeled with the knife that she had carried since her capture.

The Indians, by character, divide whatever they have with their prisoners and when a bear was killed Mary was given her share. On one occasion, Mary shot a deer with her gun and the meat from the animal was gratefully devoured by the hungry tribe members.

Over the winter, Mary Neely made several unsuccessful attempts to escape, and by the spring the journeying had resumed for the tribes, heading for most of that year in a north easterly direction towards Indiana and Detroit, Michigan. Reluctantly, Mary was dragged with them and she endured great hardships, as the weather deteriorated on the advent of a second winter.

At Michigan, the Indians camped close to a French stockade after passing through British lines and friendships were developed which led to a bartering of goods between the two groups.

It was there that Mary seized the opportunity to prepare a getaway, with the help of a Frenchman, who had befriended her and was on familiar terms with the Indian chief. The Frenchman decided on a plan which would involve giving the Indians a gallon of whisky ("fire water" to the tribes!) to drink in a container which he knew servant Mary would be tasked by the chief to return to its owner at the fort.

The Indians drank merrily and, as expected, Mary was ordered to return the vessel to its owner. It was her big chance to escape and on arrival at the stockade she was hurriedly directed to the home of the Frenchman's mother, who at first concealed her in the cellar.

When they realised that Mary had gone the Indians arrived at the stockade demanding to know where she was, but her French collaborators were not for giving her up and after spending a few days in the cellar, she was concealed in another part of the house.

Following a long period of searching the Indians eventually gave up and to ensure her safety Mary was sent to an offshore island near the Canadian borders, where 90 other people of similar plight were detained by the British as prisoners of war.

Mary's plight was just as desperate as it had been in the custody of the Indians, and the urge for complete freedom burned up in her.

After some time being spent at sea in a prison ship on Lake Ontario and Lake Chaplain, Mary saw another escape route and with two girls and an old man began heading south.

The journey was long and trying, but her incessant struggle to be free remained and after completing hundreds of miles she eventually made it to Philadelphia in Pennsylvania.

There, Mary met a family called Hiddle, who were heading for the Shenandoah Valley of Virginia via the Susquehanna River, and they agreed to let her join them on the trek, on the condition that she should help drive the stock.

The Hiddles and Mary reached their Shenandoah destination in mid-winter—Mary's third since she was taken captive—and she got lodging with a family called Spears, where she was employed as a servant. There, Mary at last felt safe from molestation by the Indians and for the first time in three years she enjoyed the luxury of sleeping in a bed.

Throughout the period of her detention Mary's brother never ceased in his search for her, although she was given up for dead by other family members. During her three-year absence Mary's mother was killed by the Indians, and several brothers, but one faithful brother kept searching in Tennessee, Kentucky and Virginia.

It was an almost impossible mission, but, luckily, while in the Susquehanna River region Mary's brother learned of a young woman who had been held captive by Indians and was now staying at the home of "the old man Spears." Mary was left-handed and her brother was able to use this as a lead to her whereabouts.

On arrival at the Spears' home, the brother was told Mary was at church. It was the Sabbath and she had gone to the morning service with Mrs Spears and her daughter. On their return, the brother immediately recognised his sister and for Mary too it was a moment of great joy, as they warmly embraced.

Within a few days Mary and her brother set out, on one horse, for Carpenters' Station in Lincoln County, Kentucky, where an older sister was waiting, and other relatives. It was too dangerous to head back to Neely's Bend in Middle Tennessee, with Indian tribes circling the region.

Mary's sister later married a son of the Spears gentleman who Mary had stayed with in Virginia. Mary's husband was also a Revolutionary soldier by the same name, George Spears, and they wed at Green County, Kentucky on February 1785.

Greene County and Lincoln County were located in a dangerous frontier region, just like Mary's former home at Neely's Creek, which her brothers re-visited and found everything destroyed, stock driven off and a scene of utter desolation.

Even the Indians had been driven off the land, to new reservations in Western Tennessee, and the less threatening situation allowed one of the Neely brothers to re-settle his father's farmlands.

Mary (Neely) Spears, during her stay with the Indians, gained a considerable knowledge of how to treat diseases in the frontier's changing climates and, seeing a great human need, this allowed her to develop a meaningful role as a physician.

She had particular expertise in dealing with white swelling (a hip disease) and chronic sores.

The reputation of Mary Neely in caring for the sick, handling the medications of the day and in service generally soon extended far and wide and her work was acknowledged by eminent doctors in Kentucky.

It was said Mary never despaired of finding a cure for the worst cases that presented themselves and, remarkably, she enjoyed a large measure of success. She was very methodical in her habits and prescribed only a minimum of medicines, contending that nature was the best remedy.

Mary had been a member of the Baptist church for most of her life and it was said her deportment was always that of a genuine Christian, showing charity to others and holding firm to the faith that had been passed on to her by God-fearing parents.

There was no church organisation in central Illinois when Mary and George settled there in the early 1820s and they and other pioneers established the Clary Grove Baptist church at their log cabin home.

It is believed to have been the first settled church in central Illinois. George Spears, meanwhile, raised a militia unit to protect the region from Indian attack and he and his men served with Andrew Jackson in the War of 1812-14 against the British.

The couple continued to live in Green County, Kentucky until 1824, when they sold up and moved to Sangamon, Illinois, then a wild and sparsely populated region. Indians still remained in the area, but they were much more peaceful and spent most of their time hunting and fishing.

Mary still practiced her "doctoring", as professional medical help was almost non-existent on this part of the American frontier in the early 19th century. She cared for patients who even travelled from Missouri and Iowa.

Some dismissed Mary as a "quack", but out of a social consciousness she felt she was doing a duty that was incumbent upon her in an isolated community she was so much a part of—to help make well those stricken with infirmity and disease.

George Spears died in 1838, after a marriage lasting more than 50 years and Mary was left with her oldest daughter and youngest son.

In 1843, Mary, by now 82, returned to Neely's Creek homestead to visit her 78-year-old brother whom she had not seen for more than 30 years and so emotional was the reunion that she stayed there for a month.

Mary (Neely) Spears was on personal speaking terms with Abraham Lincoln, later to become President. The friendship developed in the 1830s when Abraham Lincoln was resident and postmaster of Salem, Illinois.

Mr. Lincoln never tired of hearing Mary relate the experiences and deprivations of being held captive by the Indians.

Mary died in January 1852, reaching the age of 90 years, five months and 26 days. Her tragic and eventful life was indeed remarkable and, considering the terrible ordeals she came through as a young woman, it is incredible that she lived to such an age.

Mary (Neely) Spears was in the finest traditions of the American frontier woman.

References:

Sketch on the Life and Imprisonment of Mary (Neely) Spears. Nashville: Tennessee State Library and Archives.

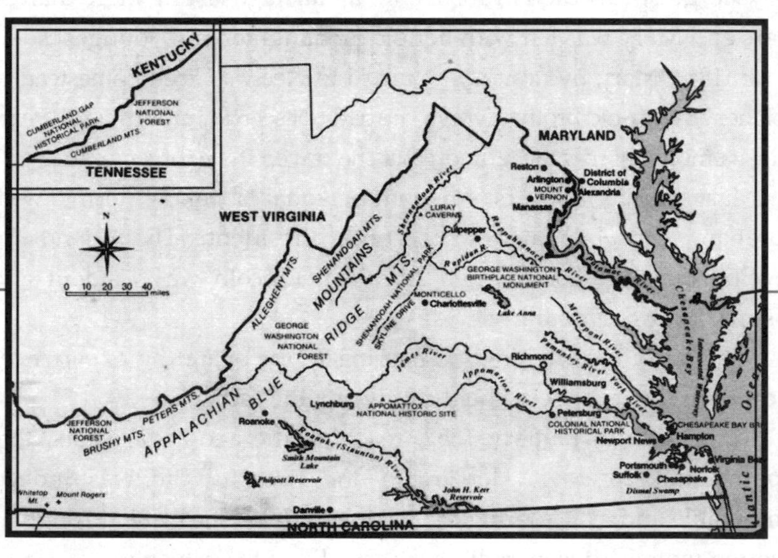
KENTUCKY
CUMBERLAND GAP NATIONAL HISTORICAL PARK
JEFFERSON NATIONAL FOREST
CUMBERLAND MTS.
TENNESSEE
N
0 10 20 30 40 miles
WEST VIRGINIA
MARYLAND
Reston
Arlington
District of Columbia
MOUNT VERNON
Alexandria
Manassas
ALLEGHENY MTS.
SHENANDOAH MTS.
MOUNTAINS
Shenandoah River
LURAY CAVERNS
Culpepper
Rappahannock River
Rapidan R.
Potomac River
GEORGE WASHINGTON BIRTHPLACE NATIONAL MONUMENT
MTS.
SHENANDOAH NATIONAL PARK
SKYLINE DRIVE
MONTICELLO
Charlottesville
Lake Anna
RIDGE
GEORGE WASHINGTON NATIONAL FOREST
Mattaponi River
Pamunkey River
York River
Chesapeake Bay
Intracoastal Waterway
Richmond
James River
BLUE
Williamsburg
Appomattox River
APPALACHIAN
PETERS MTS.
Lynchburg
APPOMATTOX NATIONAL HISTORIC SITE
Petersburg
COLONIAL NATIONAL HISTORICAL PARK
JEFFERSON NATIONAL FOREST
BRUSHY MTS.
Roanoke
Roanoke (Staunton) River
Smith Mountain Lake
CHESAPEAKE BAY BR
Hampton
Newport News
Portsmouth
Suffolk
Norfolk
Virginia Bea
Chesapeake
Dismal Swamp
Philpott Reservoir
John H. Kerr Reservoir
Whitetop Mt.
Mount Rogers
Danville
NORTH CAROLINA
Atlantic Ocean

13

Katharine (Fisher) Steel

"KATY OF THE FORT" ON THE CATAWBA RIVER

SOME WOMEN were called to give stout leadership at times of hardship and perils on the American frontier and brave Katharine (Fisher) Steel certainly was in that category.

Katharine was born in Pennsylvania of a Scots-Irish family who had emigrated from Ulster in the early 18th century and when she married Thomas Steel from the same region the couple headed for a new settlement in South Carolina.

This was about 1745, with Katharine in her early twenties, and their new home at Fishing Creek was on the eastern side of the Catawba River, which runs close to the Waxhaw and to Charlotte in Mecklenburg County.

Katharine quickly became accustomed to the ways of the frontier, labouring in the fields and in the woods with her husband to provide food and hearth for the home and learning to shoot a rifle which she accomplished with expertise.

Other settlers moved into the region from Pennsylvania and Virginia, mainly of Scots-Irish diaspora, and for survival from the elements and from attack by hostile Cherokee Indian tribes they had to co-operate closely in a tight network surrounding their log cabin homes.

The Steel home was heavily fortified as a block house, where the settlers could congregate when danger arose, and several other similar structures were erected nearby to complement the defences.

The women's role when the men folk were away from their homes either fighting the Cherokees or working in the fields was to maintain continued vigilance and raise the alarm when a threat emerged.

Katharine Steel took full responsibility for organising the women and her firmness, courage and commonsense approach provided re-assurance and real security for those who had fled their homes in a hurry to find safety in the fort houses.

Young girls were trained in the use of the rifle, for this was a life or death situation, especially if the husbands and fathers were not available in the event of a surprise Cherokee attack.

The women came together too in public worship at the nearby Waxhaw Presbyterian Church, which later became a target for the rampaging Redcoat soldiers during the Revolutionary War and where young Andrew Jackson, American President to be, and his family belonged.

Even during Sunday services a vigilant watch had to be kept in case Indians attacked suddenly and in alerts the women were always directed to the block-houses, where they would remain for days until the all-clear was given.

Thomas Steel, effectively the leader of the settlement at Fishing Creek, gained a reputation as an Indian trader who was familiar with the language of the Cherokees.

On one occasion he led a party of a dozen men to rescue seven children, who were captured by Indians after their parents (John McDaniel and his wife) were killed in a Cherokee attack on their Rocky Creek home.

At the end of a long chase, Steel's party encountered the Indians on the borders of the Cherokee territory and, after killing nearly all of them, they recovered the seven children, the eldest of whom was fifteen, and took them back to the fort houses. The children's uncle Hugh McDaniel was there to take the children into his care.

Katharine Steel kept a constant check on how the women fared and she even maintained contact with other settlements into North Carolina towards the Yadkin River. Katharine was an accomplished horsewoman and she was prepared to travel 100 miles at a time through remote and highly dangerous territory.

In 1764, Thomas Steel lost his life when he and two associates James Hemphill and Stephen White were returning from a trading expedition with the Indians. They had been away for more than a year west of the Mississippi River in the direction of New Orleans and on the way home they were way-laid by a party of Indians who stripped them of everything they had including their clothes.

Somehow, they managed to piece together some garb and one morning when they were about to resume their journey, Thomas Steel suddenly disappeared into the woods. He did not return and after some time his companions heard a gun discharged from a distance. A search was mounted, but Steel's body was never found and he was presumed dead, almost certainly murdered by Indians.

Katharine Steel was informed and, tragically left alone in a bleak wilderness with five children (three daughters and two sons). She gave not only sound motherly advice, but "fatherly" counsel and instruction to her children and wider settlement.

By 1780, Katharine's three daughters Margaret, Mary and Nancy had married, leaving the sons John and Thomas still at home with her. In the distribution of her husband's estate, Katharine divided the land and chattels equally among the children, giving each of the daughters a valuable plantation.

Katharine was admired as a high-spirited mother and a concerned community leader who made great personal sacrifices for the safety and the prosperity of the settlers on this part of the frontier.

"Katy" encouraged her sons to take up arms in the Revolutionary War. John fought against the Cherokees in several campaigns and he was also involved as a patriot militia captain at the sieges of Savannah and Charleston, and at Kings Mountain.

Thomas, the younger lad still only seventeen, was advised by his mother: "You must go now and fight the battles of our country with John." He promptly heeded the call and joined his brother at the front.

John Steel personally came to the rescue of patriot general Thomas Sumter when the general's army was posted at the Fishing Creek fort and came under attack by British dragoons commanded by General Banastra Tarleton.

Just as the British were about to pounce on the general's marquee, Steel was alerted to the danger and quickly hoisted Sumter away, together with a portmanteau containing valuable official papers. The general made it to Charlotte and John Steel's standing was enhanced in the army command.

Katharine Steel, very proud of her eldest son's military exploits, died at the old Fishing Creek fort in 1785, in her early sixties. Captain John Steel was killed in the War of 1812, by a fall from his horse.

References:

Ellet, Elizabeth F. *The Women of the American Revolution.* New York: Haskell House Publishers, 1969.

14

Elizabeth (Hutchinson) Jackson

DOUGHTY MOTHER OF A PRESIDENT

THE NATURAL responsibilities of motherhood mixed with the sense of adventure as an immigrant traveller and frontier settler and experience of real tragedy characterised the life and times of Elizabeth (Hutchinson) Jackson, mother of American President Andrew Jackson.

Elizabeth Jackson, described as an extraordinary woman, of great courage, high purpose and enormous inner strength, survived her husband Andrew's death and the loss of two sons as a result of action in the Revolutionary War.

Unfortunately, she did not live to see her youngest son Andrew rise to become a successful lawyer, soldier and national statesman.

Andrew and Elizabeth Jackson, both of lowland Scottish Presbyterian families who had settled in Ulster in the 17th century, lived for a few years of their marriage in the tiny Co Antrim hamlet of Boneybefore, a mile from the town of Carrickfergus on the shores of Belfast Lough.

The Jacksons were linen weavers, a productive occupation in the north of Ireland at the time, but, while they would have enjoyed a reasonable existence, they would not have been considered affluent.

They lived through a period of great movement from Ulster to the new lands in the American colonies and in the 1760-70 decade tens of thousands of people left the main ports of Belfast, Londonderry, Larne and Newry, bound for Philadelphia, New York, New Castle (Delaware) and Charleston.

Andrew and Elizabeth, with their sons Hugh (aged two) and Robert (six months) made the 12-mile journey from their home to the port of Larne, where they set sail for Charleston, South Carolina.

Within a short time of their arrival they had made it to the Carolina Piedmont and settled on a small plot of land at Waxhaw Creek in South Carolina, an area that was also inhabited by the Catawba Indians, considered one of the more friendly native American tribes.

Scots-Irish Presbyterians had built a church at the Waxhaw and the Jackson family was assured of a welcome as family connections (the Crawfords and McCamies) and former neighbours from Ulster had settled there.

Branches of the Hutchinson family had also settled at the Waxhaw and at Long Cane (near Abbeville in South Carolina). William Hutchinson was one of the earliest frontier settlers and the family married into the Mecklins or McLins.

Andrew Jackson Sr. had little means to feed his family, although in the less than two years of his life in America he managed to build a log cabin and produce enough crops to see them through.

The hard work took its toll and he died suddenly, of unknown causes, in March 1767, just before Elizabeth give birth to Andrew Jr.

Following a sparse funeral for her husband, Elizabeth moved to the home of her sister Jane Crawford and her husband Robert at nearby Lancaster and, on March 15, the child who was to become President was born, appropriately named Andrew after his just buried father.

Elizabeth had grand ambitions for Andrew and, indeed, her other two sons Hugh and Robert. But life was very tough in this part of the American frontier with war clouds looming; the small holding was abandoned and she took up permanent residence with the Crawfords, as a housekeeper and nurse to her ailing sister.

Described as a woman very conversive and industrious, Elizabeth Jackson was said to spin flax beautifully, her heddie yarn spinning was "the best and finest ever seen."

The boy Andrew, taught by his mother, could read at five and at eight he was able to write "a neat legible hand."

In later years, Andrew Jackson recalled long winter evenings when his mother told him and his brothers stirring tales from the Ulster homeland, of their grandfather Hugh Jackson's exploits in battle there and the oppression by the nobility of the labouring poor. These were tales celebrating courage, pride and independence.

Andrew was reported to have received a £400 inheritance from the Hugh Jackson estate back in Ulster.

Young Andrew became a hot-tempered young man, even with the saintly influences of his mother who wanted him to become a Presbyterian minister. Growing up for the first 12 years of his life in a household (the Crawfords) that was not his own, he became somewhat impatient, unsettled, and even rebellious.

Indeed, as a youth Andrew had a reputation as being wild, frolicsome, wilful, mischievous and daring. His mother, pre-occupied and wearied with work in the Crawford home, did her best to keep him on the straight and narrow, but without the guiding hand of a father young Andrew was hard to handle.

The Revolutionary War was in progress and the Jackson brothers got caught up in the struggle as the Scots-Irish settler people in the Waxhaw region virtually to a man came down on the side of the American patriot movement against the British Redcoat forces.

Elizabeth Jackson and other women of the Waxhaw used their log cabin Presbyterian church (established by the region's first Scots-Irish settlers in 1755!) as a hospital for patriot soldiers. It was attacked by revengeful Redcoat forces, who, because of the fierce patriot opposition they faced from the local settler community, saw Presbyterian meeting houses as legitimate targets.

Elizabeth's eldest son Hugh, then barely 16, joined the South Carolina militia and after engaging at the battle of Stone Ferry, he died from the excessive heat of the weather and the fatigues of battle.

It was a second tragedy for Elizabeth and her concerns were increased with other sons Robert and Andrew, a mere boy of 13, also in the militia ranks.

The Jackson boys were at the Battle of Hanging Rock and, on return to the Waxhaw, they were among forty local militiamen gathered at Waxhaw Presbyterian Church on April 9, 1781 when a company of British dragoons attacked them with sabres drawn. Eleven of the forty were captured and the church was burned down by the British.

The Jacksons were arrested by the dragoons while attempting to escape with their cousin Lieutenant Thomas Crawford and, during the initial detention, Andrew was ordered by one of the Redcoat officers to clean his boots.

The impetuous teenager bluntly refused, declaring he was a prisoner of war and required to be treated as such.

Incensed at this insubordination, the British officer promptly lifted his sword and aimed it at Andrew's head. Andrew ducked, but he still caught the force of the weapon on his head and fingers and was physically scared for the rest of his life.

With twenty other young patriot prisoners, Robert and Andrew Jackson were taken to Camden, forty miles away, and thrown into jail with 250 other prisoners.

Their prison was a hell hole of a detention centre, with no beds, no medicines and no dressing for their wounds. They contracted smallpox, much to the alarm of their mother who had followed their long trail to Camden, and Elizabeth successfully pleaded with the authorities for the boys' release, as part of the normal war-time exchange between American and British prisoners.

Robert was in very poor shape; he could not stand nor sit on horseback without support. Elizabeth managed to obtain two horses for the arduous journey back to Waxhaw, with the strapped Robert on one mount and herself on the other.

The sickly Andrew, barefooted and inadequately clothed for the atrocious weather conditions, walked the long and dangerous path home.

Tragically, Robert died within two days. Andrew was in a delirious state and it took all of Elizabeth's devotion and nursing skills, developed from years of looking after her sister Jane Crawford, to pull him through. Indeed, it was months before Andrew fully recovered.

Elizabeth, absolutely committed to a life of care, decided that Andrew was well enough for her to go to Charleston, 160 miles away, to nurse American prisoners of war held in prison ships in the harbour.

Her main concern was two nephews, but, poignantly, Elizabeth contracted cholera fever herself while tending to the sick patriot soldiers on the ships and she died after a short illness.

It was a tragic ending for such a courageous woman and, pitifully, her remains were buried in an unmarked grave in the small suburbs of Charleston. The small bundle of Elizabeth's possessions were returned to 14-year-old Andrew, only surviving member of the family at the Waxhaw. He was distraught, an orphan and sole survivor of his family.

But Andrew remembered words his mother had imparted to him: "Make friends by being honest, keep them by being steadfast; Andy…never tell a lie, nor take what is not your own, nor sue…for slander… settle these cases yourself."

For a time, Andrew Jackson lived at the homes of relatives Thomas Crawford and Joseph White before he was able to decide on his future. He was a victim of the Revolutionary War, losing his mother and two brothers in the conflict.

Their memory and the sad circumstances of their deaths were to live with Andrew Jackson for the rest of his life, right through his military career and two Presidential terms

He was determined to fulfil the high hopes that his strong-willed mother had for him and his remarkable achievement in reaching the American Presidency was in many ways attributable to the true grit and character which he had inherited from Elizabeth Jackson.

A granite monument at Waxhaw Presbyterian Church erected and looked after by Waxhaw Chapter of the Daughters of the Revolution pays fulsome tribute to Elizabeth Jackson for her extraordinary tenacity and determination in overcoming the many problems which beset the family in this part of the Carolinas during the defining period in the establishment of the American nation.

This is one of the few monuments to Scots-Irish women in the United States, which gives it a very special resonance, and the simple inscription bears testimony to the legacy to one of the outstanding women of the American frontier.

Poignantly, the gravestones of Elizabeth Jackson's two sons Hugh and Robert lie alongside the granite monument

References:

Booraem, Hendrik. *Young Hickory: The Making of Andrew Jackson*. Dallas, Texas: Taylor Publishing Company, 2001.

Degregorio, William A. *The Complete Book of US Presidents*. Avenel, New Jersey: Random House Publishing, 1984.

McPherson, James M., ed. *To the Best of My Ability: The American Presidents.* New York: Dorling Kindersley Books, 2000.

Remini, Robert V. *The Life of Andrew Jackson.* New York: Penguin Books, 1988.

Van West, Carroll, ed. *Tennessee Encyclopedia of History and Culture.* Nashville: Tennessee Historical Society, 1998.

15

Hardiness of the Ulster Women

THE SUCCESS of the Scotch-Irish settlement in the back country of America is the silent, but eloquent tribute to the hardiness of the Ulster women. It is worth noting that in all the contemporary accounts of the Ulster Plantation, the troubles with the Irish, and the establishment of the Presbyterian Church in the north of Ireland, the life and character of the women are never mentioned.

"If women are referred to at all, it is only in a census, a requirement for an oath, a casual statement that they were also present. One must conclude, by this negative evidence, that the status of women whether legal or actual, improved not a whit during the 17th century.

"No property was ever given them in the Plantation; no suits were bought for or against them at law. They were disciplined in the churches, but their life must otherwise have been the traditional one of subordination to men in a patriarchal society, doing the household work and sharing the work in the fields. Neither is there any complaint against their lot; they had never known any other.

"There were no schools for them, either in Scotland or Ulster, for they could not become ministers or attend the universities. Their only school was the hard one of being helpmeet and companion to a strong man."

References:

Leyburn, James G. *The Scotch-Irish: A Social History.* Chapel Hill: North Carolina, The University of North Carolina Press, 1962.

The Scotch-Irish were marked by family loyalty. The women led hard lives, but were patient and submission"

—Arthur Calhoun

16

Catherine Montgomery Calhoun, Rebecca Calhoun Pickens and Cateechee

THREE WOMEN DRAWN TOGETHER IN TRAGEDY

THE LONG CANE massacre of February 1, 1760 is a tragic event prominently recorded in the annals of the 18th century white settlements in the South Carolina Piedmont. There, two brave upstanding women, Catherine Montgomery Calhoun and Cherokee Indian squaw Cateechee, were to become victims in different ways in a terrible atrocity that is still recalled by people in this part of the Carolinas.

Seventy-six-year-old family matriarch Catherine Montgomery Calhoun, her son James and seven-year-old grand-daughter Catherine were among 56 white settlers killed and a number were taken captive in a vicious attack by Cherokee warriors during the French-Indian War.

Catherine Montgomery Calhoun, grandmother of leading 19th century South Carolina statesman and American Vice-President John C. Calhoun, was born in Londonderry in 1683 and she emigrated with her Co Donegal-born husband Patrick and four sons James, William, Ezekial and Patrick (John C's father) in 1733.

The family, who were to acquire considerable tracts of land in the American colonies, first settled in Lancaster County, Pennsylvania, then Albemarl, County, Virginia and, eventually, Abbeville County in South Carolina.

The Long Cane Massacre occurred as a Conastoga wagon train of 150 settlers, mostly Scots-Irish Presbyterians, were heading in the direction of Augusta, Georgia to seek fortified security refuge from an impending attack by Cherokee tribes. Others were being moved to the Waxhaw in another part of the Carolinas close to Charlotte.

It was a cold winter's morning when the families at the Calhoun settlement at Long Cane were alerted by the Indian woman Cateechee to the danger of an imminent attack.

Cateechee, risking her life, rode seventy miles on horseback to raise the alarm and the settlers made immediate preparations to travel sixty miles south to Tobler's Fort at Beech Island in New Windsor township, just across the Savannah River from Augusta, Georgia.

The journey was hampered by the weather, with the wagons getting bogged down on wet ground and, after travelling a few miles to Long Cane Creek, it was decided to make camp for the night. This was a fateful decision, for the Cherokees had arrived at the abandoned Long Cane settlement and were alerted to the camp location.

The Cherokees struck when the settlers were at their most defenceless and confusion reigned as only a few of the sixty fighting men could get hold of their guns to fend off the attack. Terrified women and children ran for cover and some became separated from the main settlement.

The attack lasted about 30 minutes and the death toll was 56 of the white settlers and 21 from the Cherokee raiding party, including their chief Sunaratehee. Five of those killed were members of the Norris family—the mother of Robert Norris, his wife, two sons and a daughter.

Grandmother Catherine Calhoun played a brave matriarchal role, even as she faced death, and attempted to shelter the children from the ravages of the attack. Several days after the massacre, her son Patrick and a militia troupe found the bodies of Catherine and 22 other victims, women and children, huddled around a large tree.

They had gathered there in a vain attempt to escape death and it was felt appropriate that they should all be buried there in a mass grave. The grave is marked by a memorial stone, erected by Patrick Calhoun to his mother. The other 33 victims were buried nearby in a second mass grave close to where they fell.

A gravestone was erected by Patrick Calhoun to his mother and, interestingly, it bore his name at the top of the monument, not hers, such was the status men had over women then.

The inscription read: "Patk Calhoun Esq. In memory of Mrs Catherine Calhoun, aged 78 years, who with 22 others, was here murdered by the Indians, the First of February, 1760."

In the several days after the massacre children were found wandering in the woods, some of them wounded by tomahawks and left for dead. Others lay on the ground, scalped but still living. It was a bloody massacre, too awful to contemplate and, tragically, part of the inevitable dangers which white settlers faced on the 18th century frontier.

The Calhouns were leading citizens of Long Cane/Abbeville, enjoying a deference and respect from the wider community. Patrick and his wife Catherine were given places of honour on public events such as Presbyterian church services, wedding and burials.

REBECCA CALHOUN, the 15-year-old daughter of Ezekiel and Jean Ewing Calhoun, was found hiding in the woods after the massacre of Long Cane on February 1, 1760.

She later became the wife of Andrew Pickens, an illustrious South Carolina patriot general in the Revolutionary War.

Pickens was, like the Calhouns, Scots-Irish and Rebecca was the mother and grandmother of South Carolina governors Andrew Pickens (1816-18) and Francis W. Pickens (1860-1862).

Being married to a senior American patriot soldier during the Revolutionary War brought grave danger for Rebecca Calhoun Pickens from the pro-British Tory forces and hostile Indian tribes. On many occasions, with her husband away on military service, she and her children was forced to abandon their home in Abbeville and move to a secret location.

It was said that Rebecca endured all "with a fortitude that never failed and true to her country, she never forgot that she was a soldier's wife."

In the Long Cane massacre, two other of the Calhoun children, Anne (Ann), four, and Mary, two, were captured and taken away to be raised by Indian squaws, but Anne was allowed to return to her family 14 years later after treaty negotiations.

Anne Calhoun learned to speak English again, but she never was able to read or write. She maintained the character of an Indian woman and wore moccasins made from the inside bark of trees. She married Isaac Matthews, a farmer, when she was 29 and they raised six children.

Three weeks after the massacre, the South Carolina Gazette in Charlestown reported: "Mr Patrick Calhoun, one of the unfortunate settlers at Long-Canes, who were attacked by the Cherokees on 1st instant, as they were removing their wives, children and best effects to safety, is just come to town and inform us that the whole of those settlers might be about 250 souls, 55 or 60 of them fighting men; that their loss in that affair amounted to about 50 persons, chiefly women and children with 13 loaded wagons and carts; that he had been at the place where the action happened, in order to bury the dead; and that he believes all the fighting men would return to and fortify the Long Canes settlement, were part of the rangers so stationed as to give some assistance and protection."

The Long Cane attack and other Indian raids in 1760 temporarily halted the flow of settlers to the Abbeville (South Carolina) and Augusta (Georgia) regions. Two days after the massacre, several hundred Cherokee Indians attacked the fort at Ninety Six in another part of the South Carolina Piedmont. The fort's surrounding buildings were burned, but the white settlers withheld the attack.

In another assault, a Cherokees attacked the Stevens Creek settlement in the Carolina Piedmont, killing twenty settlers. About 170 survivors were forced to flee to the neighbouring Fort Moore.

The barbarity at Long Cane, and other violent attacks in South Carolina, was a fall-out from the French/Indian War of 1754-63. Cherokee Indians of the upper part of South Carolina became allies of the British forces and went north with them to fight the French in Canada.

After the surrender of Quebec, these Indian warriors returned to their homes in South Carolina, and while passing through Virginia, they came into conflict with Scots-Irish settlers after taking horses. This act enraged the settlers and they pursued the Indians, killing a dozen of them.

The Cherokees were in revengeful mood by the time they reached South Carolina and several serious atrocities were committed. The white settlers retaliated and one incident led to another.

Family involvement in this tragedy and the traumas which the Calhouns faced on the Carolina frontier may explain why John C. Calhoun was such a tough conservative politician.

CATEECHEE, the young Indian women who alerted the Calhoun settlement of the Long Cane attack, was originally a Choctaw squaw who was adopted by a Cherokee chief.

Through trading contacts between the Cherokees and white settlers at Ninety Six fort in South Carolina, Cateechee became friendly with a young man called Allen David Francis and, although divided by race and culture, they pledged a life together.

However, their relationship faced obvious difficulties through the outbreak of the French-Indian War (1754-63), with Cherokee plans to attack Long Cane and Ninety Six settlements.

Cateechee learned of these after a council of war was held by the tribal leaders at Keowee Indian township and immediately she set her mind on alerting both Allen Francis and leaders of the white settlements.

Her journey on horseback on the Keowee Path towards Ninety Six and Long Cane was a highly significant event which undoubtedly saved lives, but unfortunately it could not prevent the massacre of the Calhoun wagon train members.

Cateechee and Allen Francis later married, building a cabin at Ninety Six, but they were captured and held hostage for a time at Keowee by the Cherokees for upwards a year. They managed to escape towards the Savannah River and spent a considerable time on the run from their captors, living rough in the wooded wilderness.

They eventually reached the safety of the Augusta fort and, after lying low for a period, the couple returned to Ninety Six and there they spent the rest of their lives, raising a family at a cabin known as Poplar Hill.

The legend of Cateechee and her part in alerting the white settlers at Long Cane and Ninety Six is part of South Carolina-Georgian folklore. Proof of the gallant role that she adopted is contained in a letter dated January 31, 1760, the day before the Long Cane Massacre, signed by James Francis, father of Allen Francis, at Ninety Six.

The letter related to a deposition given to him by an Indian woman which described in detail the war council at Keowee and the Cherokee intentions to attack.

References:

Burns, Hobert W. *The Life of Anne Calhoun Matthews.* Comer, South Carolina: Abbeville Books, 1996.

Edmonds, Bobby F. *The Making of McCormick County*. McCormick, South Carolina: Cedar Hill Publishing, 1999.

Fischer, David Hackett. *Albion's Seed: Four British Folkways in America.* New York: Oxford University Press, 1989.

Hurd, E. Don. *The South Carolina Up-Country.* 1981.

Salley, A. S., "The Grandfather of John C. Calhoun." *South Carolina Historical and Genealogical Magazine*, 1938.

South Carolina Gazette (South Carolina State Archives, Columbia). February 23, 1760 and March 1-8, 1760.

Waring, Alice Noble. *The Fighting Elder: Andrew Pickens.* Columbia, South Carolina, 1962.

In the Matter of Rest

Rest for hand and brow and breast,
For fingers, heart and brain;
Rest and peace! Along release,
From labour and from pain;
Pain of doubt, fatigue, despair,
Pain of darkness everywhere,
And seeking light in vain.

Peace and rest! Are they the best,
For mortals here below?
Is soft repose from work and woes,
A bliss for men to know?
Bliss of time is bliss of toil:
No bliss but this, from sun and spoil,
Does God permit to grow.

(A description of blissful toil by pioneering settlers, men and women, in the Blue Ridge Mountains of Virginia)

— by Judge Logan E. Bleckley, Rabun County, GA.
Judge Bleckley was of Scots-Irish stock.

17

Only Women at a Funeral

IN TIMES of pressing danger on the American frontier in the 18th century it was left to the women to fulfil important functions around the home while the men were away defending their territory.

Even funerals were considered not to be as important as the defence of the settlements. This was the case on the death in September, 1793 of Elizabeth Moore Carrick, wife of East Tennessee pioneering pastor the Rev Samuel Carrick, of Lebanon in the Fork Presbyterian Church outside Knoxville.

Elizabeth Moore Carrick's funeral took place on the day of a threatened attack by Indians on James White's Fort Knox (present-day Knoxville) and all the male settlers in the area, including a distraught Rev Carrick, were called upon to bear arms in defence.

This left only the women of the Lebanon in the Fork congregation to take the remains of Mrs Carrick down the Holston River in a canoe, for burial in the local cemetery.

Regrettably, such was the imminent and real danger from Cherokee Indian attack that the Rev Samuel Carrick, who was to become the first minister of First Knoxville Presbyterian Church and founder of Blount College later to become East Tennessee University, could not be present or officiate at his wife's funeral.

It was a stark life and death situation which seriously tested the resolve of the hardy settlers in this difficult terrain.

References:

Creekmore, Betsey Beeler. *Knox County, Tennessee.*

Deaderick, Lucile, ed. *Heart of the Valley: A History of Knoxville, Tennessee.* East Tennessee Historical Society, 1976.

Mack, Ashley. "For Christ in the Heart of Knoxville: History of Knoxville First Presbyterian Church."

Rothrock, Mary U., ed. *The French- Broad-Holston Country: A History of Knox County, Tennessee.* Knoxville: East Tennessee Historical Society, 1972.

18

Eliza (McCardle) Johnson

DEVOTED WIFE WHO TAUGHT HER PRESIDENT HUSBAND

ELIZA MCCARDLE JOHNSON, wife of President Andrew Johnson, was a teenage student in the small East Tennessee mountain town of Greeneville when she first met her husband.

Andrew, like Eliza of Scots-Irish immigrant stock, could not read and write and had hardly been a day at school before he met Eliza. But she taught him, romance blossomed and Andrew rose to become Mayor of Greeneville, Governor of Tennessee, a US Senator and 17th President of the United States on the assassination of President Abraham Lincoln.

Eliza McCardle, only daughter of John and Sarah Phillips McCardle, was born at Leesburg, Tennessee in 1810 and her shoemaker father died when she was a small child, leaving her to be raised on a meagre income by her mother, who was skilled at making quilts.

Local folklore in Greeneville relates that one day in September, 1826 Eliza was chatting with classmates from the Rhea Academy when she saw young Andrew, his mother Mary "Polly" (Johnson) Dougherty, her second husband Turner Dougherty and an older brother trek into the town with sparse belongings on board a little one-horse wagon.

They had just crossed the Great Smoky Mountains from the Carolinas in search of a new home and they found Greeneville on the Nolichuckey River in East Tennessee an enterprising, welcoming town, then with a population of 500.

It was love at first sight and they were married the following May—Andrew at 19 and Eliza, tall with hazel eyes, brown hair and a good figure, at 16. Eliza was modest and retiring, highly esteemed and "regarded as a model woman by all who knew her."

With Eliza's basic education at Rhea Academy, she began tutoring Andrew in reading, spelling and mathematics and, even when he acquired work as a tailor, she continued to read aloud to him in his shop. She worked hard to smooth his manners and his speech qualities.

Eliza realised that Andrew was rough around the edges but possessed a keen and engaging mind, a strong will and an unyielding Scots-Irish trait of self-determination.

The lessons eventually paid off and Andrew's stature rose as a citizen and local politician in a frontier town, largely inhabited by Scots-Irish Presbyterian residents.

He became a tailor and at the A. Johnson Tailor Shop on Main Street in Greeneville, Andrew made coats for 3.50 dollars, pants for 1.50 dollars, vests for 3.50 dollars and suits for 10 dollars.

The business flourished, with Eliza a real driving force behind her husband.

Encouraged by his wife, who helped him increase his public speaking abilities, Andrew Johnson was elevated first as a town alderman in Greeneville and then he became mayor in 1834.

By 1853 he was Governor of Tennessee and, on taking office, he immediately gave his enthusiastic backing to public education in the state. Indeed, public schools in Tennessee received funding for the first time in his first term as Governor.

Johnson was reported to have said in his later life: "If I had been educated in early life I would have been a schoolmaster. But I feel proud that I was proprietor of my own shop."

Eliza M. Johnson

Through Eliza's influence, Andrew Johnson had good reason to say "God bless women."

The marriage between Andrew and Eliza lasted for almost 50 years and they had five children (three sons Charles, Robert and Andrew Jr. and two daughters Martha and Mary -- all born in Greeneville). Ill-health plagued Eliza for a large part of her life and, although he frequently was away from home for long periods, Andrew remained a faithful husband.

Associates were convinced the relationship was an extremely happy one, the firm foundations obviously made by Eliza during the early years when Andrew required educational tutoring.

Eliza's health had deteriorated by the time Andrew had reached the White House in Washington in 1865 and she was so weakened by tuberculosis that she made only two public appearances, as a semi-invalid, during his four years of Presidential service.

Her elder daughter Martha Johnson Patterson carried out the First Lady duties and Eliza rarely emerged for public engagements from her second-floor room in the White House.

Andrew Johnson's pro-Union stance during the American Civil War alienated him from Confederate supporters in the Southern states and in the summer of 1862 his home in Greeneville was seized for use as a military hospital. Eliza had to move to the home of her daughter Mary in Carter County, Tennessee, and later to Murfreesboro in Middle Tennessee.

Despite her ailments, Eliza was very proud of her husband's rise to national recognition, as American Vice-President, and President on the assassination of President Abraham Lincoln. She had good reason to be, as her tutorship in the early years of their marriage stood Andrew in good stead.

When Andrew faced impeachment by the House of Representatives in 1868 for alleged crimes and misdemeanors in his handling of the defeated Confederacy, Eliza remained convinced of his innocence.

She predicted that the Senate trial would completely vindicate her husband, as it did, failing to get the necessary two-thirds approval.

One of their daughters Martha Patterson was hostess at White House functions and she made it clear to the President's aides: "We are plain folks from Tennessee, called here by national calamity. I trust too much will not be expected of us in a social way."

To underline the family's humble back country roots, Martha installed two Jersey cows on the lawn of the White House to supply fresh milk and butter. She even replaced the House carpets with simple muslin.

While Eliza remained in the private quarters of the White House, she still remained the matriarch of the family and, being an avid reader, she collected newspaper and magazine articles which she thought would be of interest and assistance to Andrew in fulfilling his Presidential duties.

The Johnsons returned to Tennessee in 1868, when Andrew failed to secure the Democratic Party nomination for another term, but he did resume his political career in 1874 by becoming the first President to be elected to the Senate. His health also was in decline and he did not complete his term of office.

Eliza McCardle Johnson survived her husband by only six months. She died in January 1876, aged 65, and both were buried in Greeneville, Tennessee.

Today, in Greeneville the memory of Andrew and Eliza Johnson is perpetuated at their pleasant Main Street home.

References:

Degregorio, W. A. *The Complete Book of US Presidents.* New Jersey: Wings Books, 1984.

Kunhardt Jr., Philip B., Philip B. Kunhardt III and Peter W. Kunhardt. *The American Presidents.* New York: Riverhead Books, 1999.

McPherson, James M., ed. *To the Best of My Ability: The American Presidents.* New York: Dorling Kindersley Books, 2000.

Presidents of the United States. Maryland: Coffman Publications, 1996.

Sawyer, Susan. *More Than Petticoats: Remarkable Tennessee Women.* Helena, Montana: TwoDot, 2000.

Trefousse, Hans L. *Andrew Johnson.* New York: W. W. Norton and Company, 1989.

Van West, Carroll, ed. *Tennessee Encyclopedia of History and Culture.* Nashville: Tennessee Historical Society, 1998.

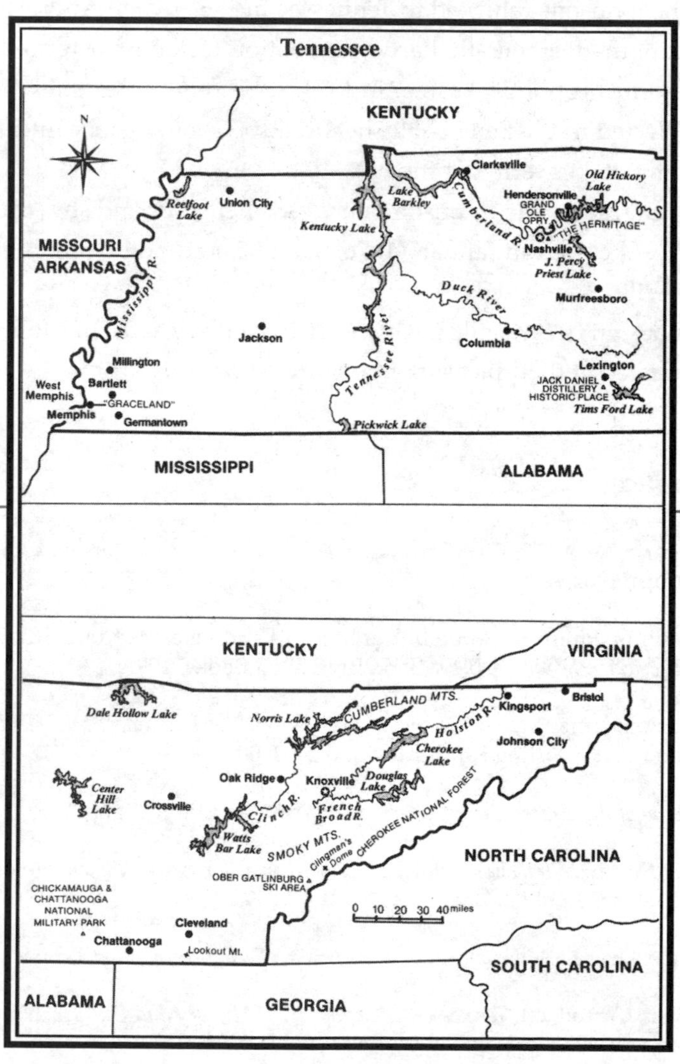
Tennessee
KENTUCKY
N
MISSOURI
ARKANSAS
Mississippi R.
Reelfoot Lake
Union City
Clarksville
Lake Barkley
Kentucky Lake
Cumberland R.
Old Hickory Lake
Hendersonville
GRAND OLE OPRY
"THE HERMITAGE"
Nashville
J. Percy Priest Lake
Murfreesboro
Duck River
Jackson
Tennessee River
Columbia
Millington
West Memphis
Bartlett
"GRACELAND"
Memphis
Germantown
Lexington
JACK DANIEL DISTILLERY & HISTORIC PLACE
Tims Ford Lake
Pickwick Lake
MISSISSIPPI
ALABAMA
KENTUCKY
VIRGINIA
Dale Hollow Lake
CUMBERLAND MTS.
Kingsport
Bristol
Norris Lake
Holston R.
Johnson City
Cherokee Lake
Oak Ridge
Knoxville
Douglas Lake
Center Hill Lake
Crossville
Clinch R.
French Broad R.
CHEROKEE NATIONAL FOREST
Watts Bar Lake
SMOKY MTS.
Clingman's Dome
NORTH CAROLINA
OBER GATLINBURG SKI AREA
CHICKAMAUGA & CHATTANOOGA NATIONAL MILITARY PARK
0 10 20 30 40 miles
Cleveland
Chattanooga
Lookout Mt.
SOUTH CAROLINA
ALABAMA
GEORGIA

19

Deborah Sampson

WOMAN IN THE FRONT LINE OF BATTLE

POSING AS A MAN in a patriot army uniform earned Deborah Sampson quite a reputation during the American Revolutionary War and so successful was the male guise she adopted that most comrades were none the wiser that this was indeed a woman.

Deborah, a heavy-boned woman five foot eight inches in height, started out as an indentured servant and eventually qualified as a teacher. But she was more attracted to soldiering and, disguised as a "Timothy Thayer", she joined the Continental Army, for adventure and a change of life.

Later in May 1782, Deborah enlisted in the 4th Massachusetts Regiment, using the name "Robert Shurtleff".

Her motivation was that soldiering was more straight-forward and interesting than farm and house work or school teaching and, dressed in a tight fitting uniform so as to hide her female attributes, she regularly warded off awkward questions from comrades deeply suspicious about her sex.

Deborah got the nicknames "Smock face" and "Molly" because of her whiskerless features, but she was a formidable lady, fearless and prepared to do anything a man was asked to do.

Deborah Sampson in the front line of battle

She resolutely marched over two weeks the long distance to West Point base in New York with her army unit and took part in a battle skirmish against the British at Tappan Sea, receiving a sabre wound on the left side of the head.

Never far from the heat of battle, she was wounded again in an engagement at East Chester and also participated in rifle action against Indian tribes at Fort Ticonderoga.

Deborah was later transferred to Philadelphia where she became an orderly to the Delaware militia and it was when she was admitted to hospital with yellow fever that her secret was discovered by a doctor treating her.

Rumours abounded about the military activities of this female volunteer, but the doctor who treated her in hospital keep her sex a secret.

However, Deborah was excommunicated by the elders of First Baptist Church of Middlesboro because she was dressing in men's clothes.

Senior military officers were informed and Deborah was exposed by some as "a fraudulent enlistee", then a serious charge at a time of war.

Word even reached General George Washington about the woman in his ranks, leading to her honourable discharge in 1783. Society in the fledgling United States was not yet ready for an army recruit from the female side and, reluctantly, Deborah had to step aside.

Deborah married a Benjamin Gannett, a farmer of Sharon, Massachusetts, and they had three children. Her war wounds continued to trouble her, however, and in 1804 she was awarded a war pension of four dollars a month as an invalided soldier, an amount that was doubled in 1818.

This woman who had infiltrated the male-dominated ranks of the army enjoyed celebrity status in some quarters and the public lectures she delivered in various states were usually followed, quite bizarrely, by her appearing in military costume to do the manual of arms.

Deborah Sampson Gannett died in 1827, aged 67, and her children were awarded compensation by a special Act of the American Congress in recognition of this "gallant soldier of the Revolution."

By American frontier standards and the mode of life at the times, Deborah was indeed a very unusual and quite remarkable person!

References:

Boatner, Mark W. III, ed. *Encyclopedia of the American Revolution.* Mechanicsburg, Pennsylvania: Stackpole Books, 1966.

Bracken, Jeanne Munn, ed. *Women in the American Revolution*. Carlisle, Massachusetts: Discovery Enterprises, 1997.

Burghardt, Renie. *History's Women: The Unsung Heroines: Deborah Sampson, A Soldier of the Revolution.*

20

Mary Ludwig Hays (McCauley)

PATRIOT HEROINE "MOLLY PITCHER"

MARY LUDWIG HAYS (McCauley) was a patriot heroine in the American Revolutionary War who was involved in direct action at the battle of Monmouth on June 28, 1778.

Molly, as Mary was known, was born at Trenton, New Jersey and was employed as a servant to Enniskillen (Co Fermanagh)-born Brigadier General William Irvine, when he was a doctor in Carlisle, Pennsylvania.

She married John Hays, who, during the War, served in the Seventh Pennsylvania Regiment, a crack unit in George Washington's army, made up almost entirely of Scots-Irishmen and commanded by Brigadier General Irvine.

With other soldiers' wives, Molly was with the regiment at the battle of Monmouth and she assisted the artillerymen by continuously bringing to the front lines drinking water in a pitcher, earning her the nickname of "Molly Pitcher."

It had been warm day and, when her husband collapsed from the heat, Molly promptly took his gun and performed heroically for the duration of the battle.

She was even unperturbed when a cannon shot passed directly beneath her legs, scorching only the bottom of her petticoat.

John Hays died in 1789 and Molly married John McCauley and during the last 10 years of her life she received a pension of 40 dollars a year, authorised by an act of the Pennsylvania legislative Assembly in February, 1822 for her heroism at Monmouth.

References:

Boatner, Mark W. III, ed. *Encyclopedia of the American Revolution.* Mechanicsburg, Pennsylvania: Stackpole Books, 1966.

Bracken, Jeanne Munn, ed. *Women in the American Revolution*. Carlisle, Massachusetts: Discovery Enterprises, 1997.

McHenry, Robert, ed. *Liberty's Women.* Springfield, Massachusetts: G & C Merriam and Company, 1980.

21

Curing Illness on the Frontier

SOME OF THE MEDICINES used to good effect by the old-tyme physicians, and passed down from one generation to another, were peculiar to the landscape and the folk traditions of the Appalachian region, some dating back to the very early frontier settlements.

Women, when no doctors or nurses were available, were invariably in the front line in tendering to the sick in their families, and in the wider community.

Some of the prescriptions used were:

- *Lemon Balm—for coughs and colds.*
- *Catnip—for colic in babies.*
- *Mint or Pennroyal—for colic in adults.*
- *Celandine—for warts.*
- *Blackberry bark and root—for diarrhoea.*
- *Pumpkin seeds—for tape worm.*
- *Oil of cloves and oil of peppermint—for toothache.*
- *Powdered Rhubarb and oil of peppermint—for heartburn.*
- *Tinc of aconite—for pleurisy.*
- *Iodide of ammonium, spirit of chloroform and syrup senega—for pneumonia.*
- *Hysocine—for whooping cough and asthma.*
- *Dover powder—for convulsion*
- *Sodium bromide and tinc foxglove—for palpitation.*
- *Dover powder, Camphor and extract of Belladena—for influenza.*

More than sixty of the herbs used to cure sickness on the early Appalachian frontier are now listed in the modern American pharmacopoeia.

22

Margaret (Cochran) Corbin

PATRIOT HEROINE "CAPTAIN MOLLY"

MARGARET (COCHRAN) CORBIN was a frontier woman in the finest tradition, performing heroics after tragedy struck members of her family twice.

As a child of four in Franklin County on the western Pennsylvania frontier during the mid-1750s, Margaret had a harrowing experience when her father, an Ulster-Scots pioneering settler, was killed by Indians and her mother taken captive.

Margaret was reared by an uncle and in 1772 she married John Corbin, a Virginian, who enlisted in the first company of the Pennsylvania artillery (George Washington's famed Pennsylvania Line).

During an attack by Hessian soldiers at the battle of Harlem Heights (Fort Washington) on November 16, 1776, John Corbin was killed and Margaret stepped forward to take over his duties as matross on a small cannon near a ridge later named Fort Tryon.

Margaret, given the title colloquially of "Captain Molly", bravely kept the gun in action as the first woman to take "a soldier's part" in the Revolutionary War.

But she was seriously wounded, with one arm nearly severed and her breast mangled by shot. With other casualties she was moved to a hospital base in Philadelphia for treatment and later parole.

Her actions were recognised by the Continental Congress in July 1779, and after being granted £30 for immediate needs, she was included on military rolls and was voted half-pay for life, with her outstanding contribution to the War effort widely acknowledged.

Margaret died, largely impoverished through an over-indulgence of alcohol, in New York state in 1800, aged 49.

However, such was Margaret's eminence in the Revolutionary War, that in 1926 her body was moved from an obscure grave to a place of honour in the West Point Cemetery.

References:

Boatner, Mark W. III, ed. *Encyclopedia of the American Revolution.* Mechanicsburg, Pennsylvania: Stackpole Books, 1966.

Bracken, Jeanne Munn, ed. *Women in the American Revolution*. Carlisle, Massachusetts: Discovery Enterprises, 1997.

Faragher, John Mack. *The American Heritage: Encyclopedia of American History.* New York: Henry Holt Incorporated, 1998.

McHenry, Robert, ed. *Liberty's Women.* Springfield, Massachusetts: G & C Merriam and Company, 1980.

23

Jane McCrea

TRAGIC VICTIM OF THE REVOLUTIONARY WAR

THE BRUTAL MURDER in 1777 of Jane McCrea, daughter of a New Jersey Presbyterian minister of a Scots-Irish background, caused bitter controversy with protagonists in the Revolutionary War.

This tall attractive young woman with long flowing blonde hair left home after her mother died and her father had remarried, moving to live with a brother who lived along the Hudson River near Saratoga.

Jane was engaged to David Jones, one of several Tories from the area to join the British Army, but this did not stop her residing alongside families who sided with the American patriots, and even sympathizing with their cause.

In the summer of 1777 when a large Redcoat force under General John Burgoyne moved down Lake Champlain and the Hudson River, Jane and a friend, Mrs. Sarah McNeil, became stranded on the wrong side of the tracks and they were captured by Wyandot Indian scouts employed by Burgoyne as an advance force.

Mrs McNeil was delivered safely into British hands at Fort Edward, but Jane McCrea was later discovered dead, with bullet wounds in her body, and scalped. She was only 23.

Death of Jane McCrea by John Vanderlyn (1804)
Wadsworth Atheneum, Hartford

Her Indian captors claimed Jane was killed by a stray bullet from an American patriot unit, but it was later established that one of the tribesmen had murdered her, probably in a drunken quarrel over whose captive she was.

When Jane's body was exhumed she was found to have three gunshot wounds, while her skull was unbroken.

The murder and the scalping produced a wave of revulsion through the American colonies and it was even raised in the House of Commons at Westminster in London, where radical MP Edmund Burke denounced the use of Indian allies for the British cause.

American general Horatio Gates was trenchant in his language of the atrocity, accusing John Burgoyne of hiring "the savages of American to scalp Europeans and the descendants of Europeans."

The killing of Jane (Jenny) McCrea, and the propaganda that ensued, had the effect of galvanising American patriot sentiment with many doubters in the frontier settlements coming out against the British and enlisting in George Washington's army.

References:

Boatner, Mark W. III, ed. *Encyclopedia of the American Revolution.* Mechanicsburg, Pennsylvania: Stackpole Books, 1966.

Harvey, Robert. *A Few Bloody Noses: The American War of Independence.* London: John Murray Limited, 2001.

McHenry, Robert, ed. *Liberty's Women.* Springfield, Massachusetts: G & C Merriam and Company, 1980.

A Proud Tennessean's Lament

Farewell to the Mountains whose mazes to me
Were more beautiful far than Eden could be;
No fruit was forbidden, but Nature had spread
Her bountiful board, and her children were fed
The hills were all garners - our herds wildly grew,
And nature was shepherd and husbandman too.
I felt like a monarch, yet thought like a man,
As I thanked the great Giver and worshipped His plan.

The home I forsake where my offspring arose;
The graves I forsake where my children repose.
The home I redeemed from the savage and wild;
The home I have loved as a father his child.
The corn that I planted, the fields that I cleared,
The flocks that I raised, and the cabin I reared;
The wife of my bosom - Farewell to ye all!
In the land of the stranger I rise or I fall.

Farwell to my country! - I fought for thee well,
When the savage rushed forth like the demons from hell.
In peace or in war I have stood by thy side,
My country for thee I have lived, would have died!
But I cast off - my career now is run,
And I wonder abroad like the prodigal son,
Where the wild savage roves, and the broad prairies spread,
The fallen - despised - will again go ahead!

—David Crockett

*These were the last verses written poignantly by Tennessee frontiersman and politician Davy Crockett. He wrote this poem in 1835 after he finished his final term in the United States Congress and before he left Tennessee for The Alamo in Texas. There he died on March 6, 1836 at the hands of Mexican assailants.

24

Cherokee Women Who Tended the Farmlands

WOMEN OF THE CHEROKEE Indian nation in the 18th century American frontier lands were the farmers in the tribes and, while the men hunted and engaged from time to time in violent conflict with the white settlers, agriculture was very much a female preserve.

In defining the woman's primary role in farming, Cherokee leaders cite the mythical tale of Selu, a woman whose name means corn and was known and revered by the tribes as the Corn Mother.

Selu testifies to the female symbolic identity and to the real-life practice of corn growing among the Cherokees and their ancestors who cultivated the Appalachian territory before the white settlers arrived.

Cherokee corn-growers, mostly the womenfolk, adjusted the crops to the climatic and soil contours of the river floodplains and hillsides and these provided solid sustenance for their people.

James Adair, a Co Antrim (Ireland)-born trader who in the mid-18th century closely studied the lifestyles and culture of the native American tribes of the south eastern region, wrote that corn was the Indians' chief produce and main dependence.

"Of this they have three sorts—the first, the smaller sort of Indian corn, which usually ripens in two months from the time it is planted; the second is yellow and flinty, which they call humany corn, and the third is the largest, of a very white and soft grain, termed bread corn."

Other foods collected by Cherokee women included nuts, fruits and grasses and these were mixed with the meats (bear, white-tail deer and small game) and the fish which came from the male hunting parties of the tribes who scoured the Appalachian mountains, rivers and lakes.

By the 18th century when the Cherokee lands of the south eastern territories were being over-run by the white European settlers the Indian tribes were adding to their diet of sweet potatoes and beans and there was even a movement into the keeping of domestic animals like pigs (hogs) and chickens.

The pigs were kept by the women and James Adair, in his detailed reports, refers to this type of farming: "Their women and children feed their pigs in small pens or enclosures through the crop-season, and chiefly on long parsley, and other wholesome weeds, that their rich fields abound with."

Pig pens, and chicken roosts were a feature of the Cherokee farm landscape in the mid-18th century. The horse was, of course a favoured animal for the Cherokee, and indeed, the other Indian tribes of the American frontier lands, but women had mixed feelings about their value.

James Adair wrote on the adverse reactions to the horse of the Cherokee women: "Around this small farm they fasten stakes in the ground, and tie a couple of split hocory, or white-oak sapplings, at proper distances to keep off the horses: though they cannot leap fences, yet many of the old horses will creep through these enclosures almost as readily as swine, to the great regret of the women, who scold and give them ill names, calling them ugly mad horses and bidding them go along, and be sure to keep away otherwise their hearts will hang sharp within them."

The Cherokees of the 18th century were more reluctant to keep cattle on their farms and the Creeks were the only tribe to really cultivate bovine herds in numbers.

Crop failure was common for the Cherokee women due to the vagaries of the Appalachian weather, particularly during winter months in the higher reaches where the tribal villages were sited. In Cherokee ideology, severe spring frosts were blamed on "a black petty God" of the north wind.

Cherokee women had higher status than any other Indian woman of the south eastern tribes and this was evident in the freedom they enjoyed in and out of marriages.

James Adair again made an interesting observation: "The Cherokees are an exception to all civilised or savage nations, in having no laws against adultery.

"They have for a considerable time been under petticoat government and allow their women full liberty to plant their brows with horns as often as they please, without fear of punishment."

Cherokee society was matrilineal, allowing the women to have an influential role in tribal warfare, government and ritual. There were a number of distinguished Cherokee women, but Nancy Ward of the Overhill Indian tribes of the Carolinas/Tennessee region was one who enjoyed the status of "beloved woman."

References:

Adair, James. *Reflections of the Lifestyles and Culture of 18th Century Native American People.* London, 1770.

Dykeman, Wilma. *Tennessee: A History*. Newport, Tennessee: Published by Wakestone Books, 1984.

Hatley, Thomas. "Cherokee Women Farmers" from *Appalachian Frontiers: Settlement, Society and Development in the Pre-Industrial Era*. Mitchell, Robert D., ed. Lexington: University of Kentucky Press, 1991.

Mitchell, Robert D., ed. *Appalachian Frontiers: Settlements, Society and Development in the Pre-Industrial Era*. Lexington: University of Kentucky, 1991.

*The Cherokee Indian language did not contain genders of masculine of feminine, but instead genders of animate and inanimate.

25

Nancy Ward

Beloved Woman of the Cherokees

NANCY WARD was a daring Indian woman from the 18th century Tennessee frontier lands who retained a strong friendship with the white settlers, particularly the Scots-Irish who were dominant in the Watauga community in the Holston region of East Tennessee.

Nanye'hi (Nancy) was born at Chota (meaning "Peace Town" or "Mother Town") in 1738, a Cherokee village on the Little Tennessee River in what is now Monroe County, Tennessee. She was the daughter of a Cherokee mother and a father, who is claimed by the Cherokees as being a Delaware Indian chief and by some historians of being of English extraction.

Nancy was described as a woman of beauty and regal presence and various compliments were paid to her by leaders of the white settler community.

James Robertson, Watauga leader and founder of Fort Nashborough (Nashville), said she was "Queenly and commanding."

Famous botanist Thomas Nuttall referred to Nancy as "tall, erect and beautiful; with a prominent nose, regular features, clear complexion, long, silken black hair, large piercing black eyes and an imperious air."

Nancy attained far-seeing leadership qualities from her uncle Attakullakulla, a Cherokee chieftain, who developed good relations with the white settlers and allowed Moravian missionaries on to Indian lands.

When Attakullakulla died in 1778, Nancy was elevated to a role as chief negotiator and peacemaker between the Cherokees and the white settlers. It was a highly sensitive time with the Revolutionary War being fought and wilder elements among the Cherokees, like Dragging Canoe, being encouraged bythe British to attack the Scots-Irish patriot settlements.

Earlier in 1775, the highly revered Nancy assumed heroine status when she took her fatally wounded husband's place in a battle between Cherokee and Creek Indian tribes. She was thereafter known as Agi-ga-u-e ("Beloved Woman"), a title carrying leadership of the woman's council of clan representatives on the Cherokee tribal council of chiefs.

Her second husband was Brian (Bryant) Ward, a white trader from South Carolina, and it was from this relationship that Nancy's strong ties with the white community were developed.

Nancy secretly warned the Watauga leader Colonel John Sevier of an impending attack by Cherokee Indians at their East Tennessee settlement on the Nolichuckey River on July 20, 1776, preventing needless death and grief to the white settlers she had come to befriend, and inevitable retaliation on her own people.

This fearless woman later that year used her prerogative as "Beloved Woman" to save a white female captive Lydia Bean, wife of a first settler of the Tennessee territory William Bean, from being burned at the stake by Cherokee warriors.

Learning of Mrs Bean's plight, Nancy broke through the crowd surrounding the mound where the burning was to take place and, after throwing aside the lighted faggots and speaking harsh words to the warriors, she led the hapless woman away.

Nancy took Lydia Bean to her home at Chota, known as the Town of Sanctuary, and there she ordered the captive to teach Cherokee

White Rose (Nancy Ward) by David Wright

From the collection of Norm & Toodie Burke

women how to make butter and cheese from the buffalo, and also show them how to set up a loom, spin thread and wool and weave cloth.

Later, when it was safe, Lydia Bean was allowed to return unharmed to her Boone's Creek home. In return for this gesture, three months later Nancy Ward's Cherokee village was spared destruction by frontier militia units as they moved to crush the Indian threat.

In 1780, Nancy Ward again gave warning of a Cherokee uprising against the white frontier settlements and she restrained the white militia groups from retaliatory action.

On several occasions, she came to the rescue of white settlers who had been captured by Cherokee tribesmen and were being sentenced to death by their captors.

Nancy made a telling contribution during negotiation of the Long Island Treaty between the Overmountain men and Cherokees in East Tennessee/North Carolina in 1781, which focused more on brokering a peace rather than the acquisition of land from the native Americans.

She cooled heated discussions with a diplomatic statement: "You know that women are always looked upon as nothing; but we are your mothers, and you are our sons. Our cry is all for peace; let it continue. This peace must last forever. Let your women's sons be ours; our sons be yours. Let your women hear our words."

Colonel William Christian, Scots-Irish leader of the Overmountain militia, replied: "Mothers, we have listened to your talk; it is humane. No man can hear it without being moved. Such words and thoughts show the world that human nature is the same vehicle everywhere.

"Our women shall hear your words, and we know that how they will feel and think of them. We are descendants of the same women. We will not quarrel with you because you are our mothers. We will not meddle with your people if they will be still and quiet at home and let us live in peace."

Nancy Ward, sometimes known as the "Pocahontas of the West", made a strong plea for Indian-white friendship at the negotiation of the historic 1785 Treaty of Hopewell.

This was the first treaty between the Cherokees and the fledgling United States authorities in the Tennessee territory and Nancy's genuine commitment to peace saved many lives, on both sides.

"We hope the chain of friendship will never more be broken," was her clarion cry.

Nancy was a strong advocate within the Cherokee nation for the adoption of productive farming and dairying methods and she was the first Cherokee cattle-owner. In her later years, Nancy and her family operated a tavern for travellers along the Ocoee River in East Tennessee.

For much of her life, Nancy tried to resist the white designs on Indian lands by urging the tribal leaders not to sell, but she had little success and, gradually, Cherokee influence on the historic Tennessee lands was eroded. She died in 1822, aged 84 and is buried at Benton, Tennessee.

The grave, looked after by the Nancy Ward Chapter of the Daughters of the American Revolution, carries the inscription: "In memory of Nancy Ward, Princess and Prophetess of the Cherokee Nation. The Pocahontas of Tennessee. The constant friend of the American Pioneer."

Nancy's daughter Betsy married General Joseph Martin, who later became Virginia's Indian agent to the Cherokees, and another daughter Nannie, married Richard Timberlake, a descendant of the explorer and trader Henry Timberlake.

Some have very unfairly tried to portray Nancy Ward as a traitor to her Cherokee people, but this was certainly not the case.

Nancy fully accepted that the native American tribes were unable to counter the knowledge and expertise of the white settlers and it was said she struggled desperately to save her people from the tragedy which were to hit their homes, towns, and nation, culminating in the disastrous Trail of Tears to Oklahoma by the various tribes in the early 1830s.

A fond expression by Nancy Ward which gives testimony to her life and sacrifice for peace was: "The white men are our brothers, the same house shelters us, the same sky covers us."

References:

Calloway, Brenda. *America's First Western Frontier.* Johnson City: The Overmountain Press, 1989.

Crutchfield, James A. *Tennesseans at War.* Nashville: Rutledge Hill Press, 1987.

McHenry, Robert, ed. *Liberty's Women.* Springfield, Massachusetts: G & C Merriam and Company, 1980.

Sawyer, Susan. *More Than Petticoats: Remarkable Tennessee Women.* Helena, Montana: TwoDot, 2000.

Van West, Carroll, ed. *Tennessee Encyclopedia of History and Culture.* Nashville: Tennessee Historical Society, 1998.

26

Rebeckah (Meek) Kennedy

Patriot Woman Who Took Real Risks

HEADS of American frontier families were normally the men, who took the risks, provided the food, shelter and ensured their kin was adequately defended.

Rebeckah (Meek) Kennedy was an exception and when she was widowed in the north of Ireland in 1788 through the death of her military medical doctor husband Samuel, she assumed responsibility as matriarch of her wider family.

This stout-hearted lady decided on emigration to America from the home in Londonderry and, with seven of her nine children—two married daughters stayed behind in Ireland—she crossed the Atlantic to follow the path of her grandfather Adam Meek to North Carolina via Charleston.

Eventually, she worked his way through the wilderness along the Holston River to Jefferson County in East Tennessee.

Some time about 1790, Rebeckah, with her seven children chose a log cabin on a creek bank orchard in Knox County, Tennessee and the home was a quadrant of a frontier fortification known as White's Fort, which was on the site of the present-day city of Knoxville.

It was a tough existence for Rebeckah and her family with the rigours faced in a bleak environment and constant danger from Cherokee Indian tribes who menacingly roamed the area, but they survived and Rebeckah died in Knoxville in 1815, content that sons and daughters and their offspring were firmly established and prosperous in frontier society.

Adam Meek was a militia captain in the Revolutionary War and family members made it Kentucky, settling at Big Sandy Valley in Johnson County.

References:

Wood, Mayme Parrot. *Hitch Hiking Along the Holston River.* Nashville: Richland Press, 1964.

27

Upholding Women's Rights in a Western State

WYOMING was an American state which was far advanced in its treatment of women, with legislation passed in 1869 giving females in the territory the right of suffrage, and to hold civic office.

An act passed by the Territorial Assembly declared: "That every woman of the age of twenty-one years, residing in this territory, may, at every election to be holden under the laws thereof, cast her vote and her rights to the elective franchise and to hold office shall be the same under the laws of the territory, as those of electors."

The vote for women in Wyoming was 50 years before female suffrage was added to the United States Constitution.

The aim of legislators in this isolated western state was to attract responsible women settlers, to offset the influence of lawless male elements who had arrived to work on the railroads.

Leading campaigner Esther Hobart (McQuigg) Morris was the first woman to hold office in Wyoming, becoming a justice of the peace in South Pass City in 1870.

Esther Morris emerged as a symbol for the women's rights movement across America and she was elected Wyoming's representative in Statuary Hall in the Capitol Building in Washington DC.

Later, in 1923-25, Nellis Tayloe Ross was elected as Wyoming's first and only woman Governor. She was a teacher who assumed the Governor's role on the death of her husband William B. Ross.

Women held many administrative posts in Wyoming down the years, particularly in the management of charitable institutions like hospitals and children's homes.

References:

Hallberg, Carl. "Women's History in Wyoming." Wyoming State Archives.

Lewis, Jon E. *The Mammoth Book of the West: The Making of the American West.* London: Robinson Publications, 1996.

In American frontier society, gossipy women were permitted the practice, but with a distinct understanding that recognised groups were not to be taken seriously. However, if a man doubted the veracity of another and called him a liar, inevitably it led to a fight if the abused man was to save his reputation with very often death from the resultant duel.

28

Nancy (Morgan) Hart

FORMIDABLE WOMAN WITH REAL COURAGE

NANCY (MORGAN) HART was another of the legendary American Revolutionary War heroines who put the fear of God into those who confronted her.

This six-feet tall, very muscular woman was born on a frontier settlement in 1735 and married Benjamin Hart, a Virginian by whom she had eight children. The family lived in South Carolina for a time, before settling at Wilkes county in Georgia.

Nancy could handle a long rifle as good as any man and as a supporter of the patriot cause she got caught up in some fierce confrontations with British-backed forces and Indians, both on the battle front and behind the lines as a scout, dressed up as a man.

On one occasion, six enemy Tory soldiers from Augusta entered her log cabin home and ordered a meal. As they sat drinking whiskey which Nancy had plied them with, she sent her 12-year-old daughter Sukey off to warn her husband of the danger.

She then erected two muskets through a hole in the wall and took aim at the soldiers from a third weapon in her hand.

Nancy killed one Tory who rushed her and wounded another and with the three weapons she held off the soldiers until her husband arrived with a posse of men. The surviving soldiers were taken to the woods and hanged.

Nancy Morgan Hart capturing Tories attacking her home

On a particular spying mission, Nancy crossed the Savannah River on a raft of logs tied with grapevines and she brought back valuable information for the patriots. Nancy lived in several areas of Georgia, but after her husband's death she moved to Kentucky, where she died in 1830, aged 95.

References:

Boatner, Mark W. III, ed. *Encyclopedia of the American Revolution.* Mechanicsburg, Pennsylvania: Stackpole Books, 1966.

McHenry, Robert, ed. *Liberty's Women.* Springfield, Massachusetts: G & C Merriam and Company, 1980.

29

Betty Zane

CELEBRATED HEROINE OF WEST VIRGINA

BETTY ZANE enjoys an honoured place in West Virginian folklore for her heroics against attacking Indians at Wheeling, the township founded by her brothers Ebenezer, Jonathan and Silas.

It was September, 1782 and 16-year-old Betty had just returned from school in Philadelphia when the family homestead came under attack from native American tribesmen.

The alarm was raised and all of the inhabitants of the locality hurriedly crowded into the adjacent Fort Henry, but they did not have time to secure a supply of gun powder from the magazine in Colonel Ebenezer Kane's fortified home some 50 yards away.

Betty volunteered to fetch more from her brother's house and, resisting objections that a man could run faster, she is reported to have said: "You have not one man to spare; a woman will not be missed in the defense of the fort. Tis better a maid than a man should die."

She dashed for the house, much to the amazement of the attacking Indians, who shouted "Squaw, Squaw", and did not fire. However, when she re-appeared from the house with a supply of powder, they opened up and although Betty's clothes were pierced no bullets struck her and remarkably she made it back to the fort safely.

Betty Zane
Courtesy of Ohio County Public Library

Thankfully, the powder was enough for those manning the fort to hold out until reinforcements arrived.

The Zanes, who took part in the first explorations of Kentucky with Daniel Boone, were former Quakers of Danish extraction and Ebenezer, with his brothers, established Wheeling in 1770. In Dunmore's War of 1774, Ebenezer was disbursing agent for the Virginia militia.

In 1796 Ebenezer Zane got permission from the United States Congress to open a road from Wheeling to Limestone (Maysville), Kentucky, known as Zane's Trace, when southern Ohio was opened for settlement by the Treaty of Greenville.

References:

Boatner, Mark W. III, ed. *Encyclopedia of the American Revolution.* Mechanicsburg, Pennsylvania: Stackpole Books, 1966.

McHenry, Robert, ed. *Liberty's Women.* Springfield, Massachusetts: G & C Merriam and Company, 1980.

30

Ann (Hennis) Bailey

FEARSOME FRONTIER SCOUT AND SOLDIER

LIVERPOOL (England)-born Ann (Hennis) Bailey was a frontier scout, messenger, spy and Indian fighter who emigrated as a 19-year-old to America in 1761, believed as an indentured servant.

Ann's first husband Richard Trotter was a Shenandoah Valley, Virginia settler, who, after serving as a militiaman under general Braddock through the French-Indian War of 1754-63, was killed at the Revolutionary battle of Point Pleasant in October, 1774.

Upon Trotter's death, Ann, seeking revenge for her husband's death, adopted male dress, took up a rifle, tomahawk and a butcher's knife and actively involved herself in the violent conflicts of the frontier.

This stout, short but formidable lady, who wore a petticoat over her buckskin breeches, left her young son with a friend and neighbour and went on the warpath.

Ann was a crack shot, a superb horsewoman and at woodcraft it was said she was as expert as any white man or Indian. She could even use her fists to box in a threatening manner.

Her fearsome reputation on both sides of the white settler / Indian divide earned her the title of the "white squaw of the Kanawha" or

"Mad Ann." She could "out-ride, out-shoot, out-tomahawk" any man, red or white, and her fearsome reputation was recognised by the Indian adversaries.

Ann's most famous feat of daring and skill was in 1789 when she helped save Fort Lee, an isolated outpost on what today is Charleston in West Virginia. She slipped through the lines of Indians and, riding 100 miles to Savannah, brought back a very necessary supply of gunpowder. Her action saved a massacre of the white settler families holed up in the fort.

In 1788 Ann and her second husband John Bailey moved to "Clendenin's Settlement" or Fort Lee on the site of present-day Charleston in West Virginia and in 1791 when Indians laid siege to the fort in 1791 this gallant Liverpudlian had her finest hour.

Ann volunteered to ride for help when the settlers' powder ran low and, after dashing from the fort through lines of Indian tribes, she rode for one hundred miles to Fort Union (present-day Lewisburg) and was back in three days with fresh supplies.

The situation was retrieved thanks to the initiative of this exceptional frontier woman, who died in Ohio in 1825, aged 83.

References:

Harkness, David J. "Colonial Heroines of Tennessee, Kentucky and Virginia." Compiled by University of Tennessee, 1974.

McHenry, Robert, ed. *Liberty's Women.* Springfield, Massachusetts: G & C Merriam and Company, 1980.

31

Lydia Barrington Darragh

AIDE TO GEORGE WASHINGTON'S ARMY

DUBLIN-BORN Lydia Barrington Darragh is credited in American revolutionary folklore with saving George Washington's army at a crucial point in the war.

Lydia emigrated to America with her teacher husband William Darragh in 1753, settling in Philadelphia at a time when radical politics was re-shaping life in the colonies with the demise of the pacifist Quaker establishment to be replaced by a more strident Scots-Irish-influenced new order.

During the British occupation of the Pennsylvania capital, General William Howe had his headquarters opposite the Darragh home and opportunity presented itself for Lydia on December 2, 1777 when Howe's adjutant general and other Redcoat officers commandeered one of her rooms for a secret conference.

Lydia, listening at the keyhole, learned of the imminent plan to attack George Washington at Whitemarsh, eight miles away and, hastily making an excuse that she needed flour from a nearby mill, she furtively obtained a pass to leave the city.

She headed for Whitemarsh, passed the news on to a friend Colonel Thomas Craig and returned to Philadelphia, with a sack of flour.

Whereupon, when the British forces marched on Whitemarsh they found George Washington's Continental Army ready for battle and this resulted in General Howe and his men having to make a speedy hasty retreat.

Lydia Barrington Darragh became a respected businesswomen in Philadelphia and left a sizeable estate.

References:

Bracken, Jeanne Munn, ed. *Women in the American Revolution*. Carlisle, Massachusetts: Discovery Enterprises, 1997.

McHenry, Robert, ed. *Liberty's Women.* Springfield, Massachusetts: G & C Merriam and Company, 1980.

32

Betsy Ross

DESIGNER OF THE STARS AND STRIPES

BETSY ROSS is the woman credited with manufacturing in 1776 the first flag for the United States of America. The Stars and Stripes emblem, which Betsy designed in the back parlour of her home on the invitation of General George Washington, was adopted by the American Continental Congress.

The Betsy Ross flag was designed with 13 five-pointed white stars in a circle within the Blue Union and with seven Red and six White stripes.

Betsy (Elizabeth Griscom) was born in Philadelphia into a family of English extraction and she was brought up as a Quaker. But upon her marriage to John Ross, an Episcopalian and a friend of George Washington, she was disowned by the Society of Friends.

John Ross, an upholsterer by trade and, like his wife a strong American patriot, died in January, 1776 from injuries received when gun-powder he was guarding at ammunition stores on the Delaware River exploded.

Betsy was widowed at 24, but she carried on the upholstery business and became an even more fervent supporter of American independence, receiving a nickname from British soldiers of the "Little Rebel."

It is recorded that in June 1776, Betsy Ross was authorised by a senior committee of the American Continental Congress, which included patriot commander-in-chief General George Washington and her uncle by marriage Colonel John Ross, to design a flag for the embryonic nation.

Betsy Ross discussing the design of the flag with George Washington

General George Washington, it is claimed, personally drew up the design for the flag and Betsy had the finished article ready within days for approval by the Continental Congress.

Other designs were considered, but Betsy's is the one which was accepted, although other variations of the Stars and Stripes were in vogue over the ensuing years and there are some historians who would dispute that Betsy's flag became the official emblem.

Betsy's initial order was the fore-runner for flags and emblems which she continued to make for the United States federal government for the next 50 years. Betsy Ross died in 1836.

References:

Boatner, Mark W. III, ed. *Encyclopedia of the American Revolution.* Mechanicsburg, Pennsylvania: Stackpole Books, 1966.

History's Women: The Unsung Heroines. Lexington, Virginia: History of Augusta County.

McHenry, Robert, ed. *Liberty's Women.* Springfield, Massachusetts: G & C Merriam and Company, 1980.

33

Mary Patton

GUNPOWDER MAKER FOR THE FRONTIER PATRIOT MILITIAS

MARY PATTON became a heroine in the Appalachian back country for the daring role she played as gunpowder maker for the American patriots during the Revolutionary War.

Mary McKeehan was English-born of Scottish parentage and she married Ulster Presbyterian settler John Patton in 1772 when their families were living in eastern Pennsylvania and he was a private in the local militia.

Her father David taught Mary the art of powder-making when they lived in England and she passed the skills on to her husband John in his role as a militia man and general merchant.

At the start of the Revolutionary War, John and Mary moved with their two children from Cumberland County, Pennsylvania to the Overmountain region of Sycamore Shoals-Elizabethtown in North Carolina, which today is part of the state of Tennessee.

There, in partnership with another Scots-Irish settler Andrew Taylor, they established a gunpowder mill along the lines of the operation they ran at Carlisle township in Pennsylvania and found a ready business with the local militia, of which Taylor was connected.

Mary, looked upon as a redoubtable woman of steely character and courage, became a celebrated folk heroine of the hardy Overmountain settlers in the Tennessee/North Carolina territory. She was held in the highest esteem for the role she played in the War.

On one occasion when she was returning home alone on horseback, after delivering a consignment of black powder, a masked man rode out in front of her and demanded her money. She promptly said that her husband was some distance behind, carrying the money, and when the bandit hesitated Mary spurred her horse and reached home safely.

On her trips, Mary would shoe the horse herself and when the journey was complete she would remove the shoes to save them for another day.

After the Revolutionary War, Mary continued to make the gunpowder for militia units, riding as far as South Carolina, Virginia and Georgia to sell the powder for about a dollar a pound. She was a real expert when it came to powder making, simply with the use of a large black kettle and the relevant substances.

The processes in the manufacture of black gunpowder were the production of saltpeter and charcoal and in the thriving cottage industry operation of the Patton household mill much hand labour was needed.

The powder was packed in lots of 25, 50, 100 pound kegs and transported to the battle lines on horse-drawn carts.

Mary supplied 500 pounds of black gunpowder to the 850 Overmountain militia soldiers from Sycamore Shoals, who fought at the Battle of Kings Mountain in South Carolina on October 7, 1780.

Her highly potent mix was an essential ingredient in securing a highly significant victory over the British Redcoats for the Overmountain Men, who consisted mainly of Scots-Irish settler farmers from the Watauga community in the North Carolina/Tennessee territory.

Robert, Thomas and Matthew Patton, all from a Scots-Irish background, are listed as having fought at the Battle of Kings Mountain—a decisive encounter for the American patriots in the War.

Mary Patton taught other members of her family and the wider kin to manufacture gun-powder and the celebrated Patton mill continued in production for upwards of a century to the latter half of the 19th century. The land on which the powder mill was situated stayed in the family under the early 1960s.

Gun-powder supplies from the Patton mill were used by the Confederate Army units in the Appalachian states during the American Civil War.

A large black kettle, belonging to Mary Patton for use in her powder-making, is a prized artifact of the Massengill Museum of the Overmountain History at Rocky Mount in North East Tennessee.

Mary Patton died on December 15, 1836, aged 85, and she is buried on Tennessee soil in the Patton-Simmons Cemetery at Sycamore Shoals near Johnson City.

References:

Howard, Robert A. and E. Alvin Gerhardt Jr. *Mary Patton: Powder Maker of the Revolution.* Tennessee: Rocky Mount Historical Association, 1980.

Van West, Carroll, ed. *Tennessee Encyclopedia of History and Culture.* Nashville: Tennessee Historical Society, 1998.

N
A
D
A
L. Superior
L. Michigan
L. Huron
L. Ontario
L. Erie
MICHIGAN
NEW YORK
MAINE
VERMONT
NEW HAMPSHIRE
Monmouth
Londonderry
Boston
MASS
Worcester
CONN
Hudson R.
New York
Princeton
N.J.
Philadelphia
Harrisburg
Donegal Springs
Hanna's Town
Pittsburgh
Cleveland
PENNSYLVANIA
Susquehanna R.
Potomac R.
MD
Washington
DEL
Shenandoah R.
VIRGINIA
W. VIRGINIA
Charleston
Staunton
OHIO
INDIANA
ILLINOIS
Bloomington
St Louis
Ohio R.
Mississippi R.
Platte R.
KANSAS
MISSOURI
OKLAHOMA
ARKANSAS
KENTUCKY
Lexington
Cumberland Gap
Cumberland R.
Nashville
TENNESSEE
Tennessee R.
APPALACHIAN MOUNTAINS
BLUE RIDGE MOUNTAINS
NORTH CAROLINA
King's Mt
Waxhaw
SOUTH CAROLINA
Charleston
GEORGIA
ALABAMA
MISSISSIPPI
LOUISIANA
New Orleans
San Jacinto
GULF OF MEXICO
N
Key:
Areas of concentrated Scots-Irish settlement 1720-1800
Areas with significant Scots-Irish population 1800-1860
0 250 500 km
0 100 200 300 miles

34

Margaret Catherine (Kate) Barry

CAROLINA HEROINE OF THE WAR

MARGARET CATHERINE (KATE) BARRY, from Walnut Grove, Spartanburg, South Carolina, was one of the outstanding heroines of the Revolutionary War for the part she played in saving lives at the Battle of Cowpens in January, 1781.

Kate Barry was the daughter of Co Antrim couple Charles and Nancy Barry Moore, who emigrated to America about 1750. She was a hardy resolute woman, married at 15 to Captain Andrew Barry, who came from a Scots-Irish family that had settled in the Tyger River region of the South Carolina Piedmont.

Andrew Barry was an officer in the South Carolina Rangers during the War and he commanded militia companies at the battles of Fishing Creek, Musgrove's Mill (where he was wounded!) and at Cowpens.

The couple had eleven children, five sons and six daughters and, notwithstanding her role in the home, Kate performed duties as a volunteer scout and guide for the South Carolina patriots, always acting in support of her husband.

The scouting operations centred mainly in Spartanburg County, and, being an excellent horsewoman, she was able to cover the thick wooded terrain and Indian trails with remarkable speed of movement.

Kate frequently rode to where the militia was camped to warn of impending danger, and, with the help of a black slave, Uncle Cato, she completed many successful scouting operations.

Hollow trees would be filled with corn to provide against food shortages and, very often, after raids by British forces, settler homes were left destitute and the corn caches in the trees were used to feed the people and the animals.

Smuggled goods were also concealed in the women's clothes through enemy lines to the patriots, either on the battle fields or in prison. It was a rouse that was sometimes spotted by alert British soldiers who noticed the women periodically changed from a stocky build to being thin, or vice versa.

This highly motivated frontier woman even engaged in rounding up militia troops when reinforcements were required. At the battle of Cowpens she took responsibility for gathering up patriot groups and moving them to strategic points in the frontline of battle.

Andrew Barry was holding the line with Scots-Irish general Andrew Pickens against the British Redcoat troops under the command of Banastre Tarleton, a Merseysider from the North of England, who was a much reviled figure in the Scots-Irish Carolina communities of Charlotte and Waxhaw.

As battle ensured at Cowpens, the women of Nazareth Presbyterian Church, 13 miles away, were anxiously assembled in a house near the church and a vigilant Kate Barry was at the shoals on the Tyger River, waiting for reports from the battlefield. When news of the crushing victory for the patriots was passed along she rushed to the church to inform the women, who were much relieved by the news.

At Cowpens, 926 of Banastre Tarleton's troops were killed, captured or wounded and many armaments taken. On the American side, 132 were killed and 60 wounded.

On another occasion, when the British led by "Bloody Bill" Cunningham made an infamous raid into the area, Kate heard them across the river near her father's home at Walnut Grove. She tied her two-year-old daughter Catherine (Little Katie) to a bed post for safety and rode to her husband's company for help. The action forced the British to retreat.

Once, when the Redcoats came to Kate's home, demanding to know the whereabouts of husband Andrew's company, she refused to co-operate and was tied up and struck three times with a leash. The attack angered the men of her husband's company, for it was said that any one of them would have given his life for Kate.

Again on another front, Kate Barry, with the British in hot pursuit, swam her horse across the Pacolet River near Hurricane Shoals. Fortunately, the water rose to a high level, just as Kate and the horse reached dry land on the other side, thus preventing the British from capturing her and the important message she carried.

The heroic deeds of Kate Barry became part of South Carolina folklore for more than 200 years and today her memory is revered by many people in the Spartanburg and Greenville areas.

Kate's nephew was Senator William Taylor Barry, who was President Andrew Jackson's Postmaster General in the White House after soldiering with Jackson in the War of 1812-13. He was also United States minister to Spain.

References:

Miller, Mary Montgomery. "Kate Barry." Moore, South Carolina: History of Nazareth Presbyterian Church.

THE CONFEDERATE STATES OF AMERICA: 22 FEBRUARY, 1862
DEO VINDICE

35

Women Sign up for the Confederacy

TENNESSEE has long been renowned as the "Volunteer" state and it was there, during the American Civil War of 1861-65, that a girls' company of the Confederate Army was formed.

The female unit was set up in Rhea County, one of only three counties in East Tennessee which backed the Confederacy. The region was generally pro-Union in sympathy, even though it was part of a Southern state, with Middle Tennessee and West Tennessee solidly backing the Confederates.

The Confederate counties were under constant danger with Union soldiers encamped all around them and marauders roaming the hills, seizing what they could.

To counter the threat, the young women of Rhea County, mostly aged 16 to 17, decided in the autumn of 1862 to organise in support of male relatives and boy friends fighting for the Confederacy, with most of the activity centred on the town of Washington.

Secret meetings were held in a local church and, divided into "squads", the "Rhea County Spartans" set about visiting the companies of their fathers, brothers, and boy friends, bringing clothing, food, and other essentials to them.

The girls were not directly involved in the fighting, but they had a chain of command, running through from captain to lieutenants, sergeants and privates, and they provided an effective counter to the Union military presence in the region.

The company operated until the end of the War in 1865, when defeat for the Confederate Army made it very difficult to continue.

During the Civil War, women were prominently involved in the sanitary commission, which gathered and delivered medical and food supplies from every town and village in the Northern states to the Union Army. Women in the South operated on a similar basis for the Confederacy.

References:

Broyles, Betty J. *History of Rhea County, Tennessee.* Tennessee: Rhea County Historical and Genealogical Society, 1991.

Faragher, John Mack. *The American Heritage: Encyclopedia of American History.* New York: Henry Holt Incorporated, 1998.

* Female units existed in other parts of Tennessee during the Civil War, with one pro-Union group known as the Blount County Guards.

36

Elizabeth Paxton Houston

MOTHER OF A GREAT AMERICAN LUMINARY

ELIZABETH PAXTON HOUSTON, mother of Tennessee and Texas Governor Sam Houston, was made of a steely resolve needed for the arduous frontier life in the Shenandoah Valley of Virginia and East Tennessee during the late 18th century and early 19th century.

This mother of nine children—six sons and three daughters of which Sam was the fifth- was a member of a Scots-Irish family—the Paxtons, which, like the Houstons, moved from the north of Ireland to America during the mid-18th century.

Elizabeth was a very devout Presbyterian, who according to records of the time was "gifted with intellectual and moral qualities" above that of most women on the frontier. It was said her life was characterised by "purity and benevolence."

During the Revolutionary War, Sam Houston's father Sam had served as captain, paymaster and later major in Morgan's Rifle Brigade, a crack unit of the American patriot army and in 1783 he married Elizabeth Paxton, a daughter of one of the richest men in the Shenandoah Valley.

Sam, Sr. inherited his father's farm at Timber Ridge outside Lexington and they worshipped at Timber Ridge Presbyterian Church along with other Scots-Irish settler families. In 1776, Sam donated

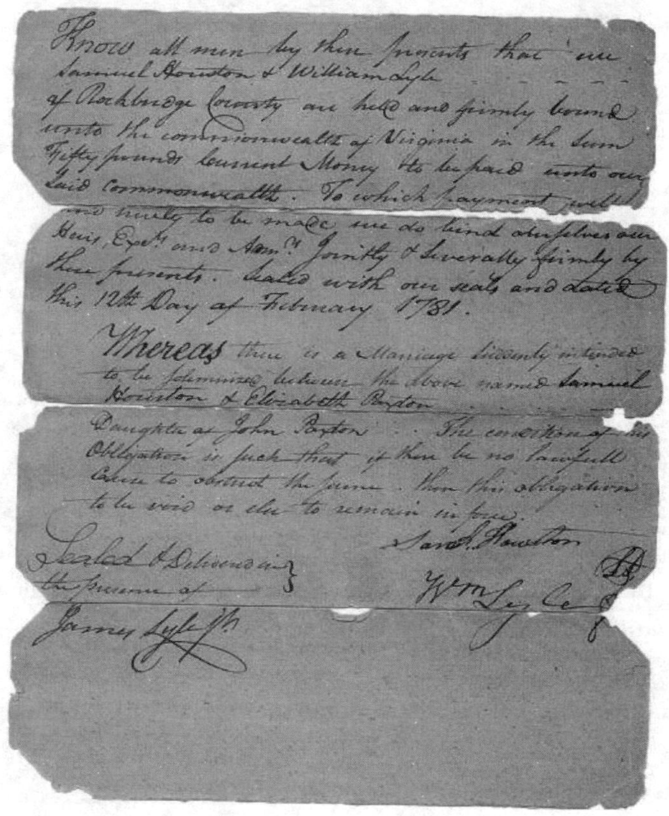

Know all men by these presents that we Samuel Houston & William Lyle of Rockbridge County are held and firmly bound unto the commonwealth of Virginia in the Sum Fifty pounds Current Money to be paid unto our said commonwealth. To which payment well and truly to be made we do bind ourselves our Heirs, Exec^rs and Adm^rs Jointly & Severally firmly by these presents. Sealed with our seals and dated this 12th Day of February 1781.

Whereas there is a Marriage suddenly intended to be solemnized between the above named Samuel Houston & Elizabeth Paxton Daughter of John Paxton. The condition of this Obligation is such that if there be no lawfull Cause to obstruct the same then this obligation to be void or else to remain in force.

Saml. Houston

Sealed & Delivered in the presence of James Lyle Jr.

Wm Lyle

Marriage bond between Elizabeth Paxton and Sam Houston, Sr.

land for the establishment of an academy in Lexington run by the Presbyterian church to be known as Liberty Hall, and later to become the Washington and Lee University.

When her husband Sam, a major in the Virginia militia, died in 1807 on a tour of frontier army posts, Elizabeth Houston, then aged 52, moved with her family from Lexington in the Shenandoah Valley in a covered Conestoga wagon train to Maryville, Blount County in the Great Smoky Mountains of East Tennessee.

There, they settled on land which Sam Sr. had purchased with the intention of moving closer to kinsfolk who had settled in East Tennessee.

They worshipped at Baker's Creek Presbyterian congregation and twice and often three times a week Elizabeth and the children walked in all weathers the four miles over the hills to services. They were also attached to New Providence Presbyterian Church in Maryville.

Sam and his brothers helped their mother erect the log cabin home on a 419-acre site at Maryville, at a point close to a river which divided the settlements of the white settlers from the lands of the Cherokee Indians.

The land was cleared, the house was built and the crops were planted, in typical late 18th and early 19th century frontier style and, with the children grouped all around her, Elizabeth proved a redoubtable industrious citizen of Maryville and its environs, even taking a keen interest in the business affairs of the town by opening a grocery and hardware store.

Elizabeth Houston had shown remarkable courage and determination in moving the large family household such a distance after the death of her husband. She was a woman of big build and forceful personality, qualities that stood her in good stead in the male-dominated world of the Virginia-Tennessee frontier.

Elizabeth Houston's sound Christian counseling was an obvious influence on young Sam and in later life he admitted that the early impressions passed on by her far outlived all the wisdom of his adult life.

Sam adored his mother. She had nursed him from a serious injury he had received during a battle with the Indians and on the little finger of his left hand he wore a ring which she had given as a young man. The ring had the word "Honor" engraved on it.

Sam, in one of his nostalgic moments in 1859 four years before his death and long after his mother had passed on, said: "Sages may reason and philosophers may teach but the voice which we heard in infancy will ever come to our ears, bearing a mother's words and a mother's counsels."

The renowned early 19th century soldier, statesman and politician was a complex man who did not always live up to the fine Christian principles set by his mother, but he did, however, end his days as a Baptist convert, largely through the steadying influence of his second wife, Margaret Lea.

In August 1831, Sam Houston was involved in important land treaty talks with the Indian tribes when he heard that his mother was very ill and dying. He rushed immediately to Maryville in East Tennessee to be with her and arrived just in time.

Elizabeth Paxton Houston was in her last hours and it was a defining moment in Sam's life as the woman who had most influenced him left the scene of time.

References:

Haley, James J. *Sam Houston.* Norman, Oklahoma: Oklahoma University, 2002.

Harper, Herbert L., ed. *Houston and Crockett : Heroes of Tennessee and Texas: an Anthology*. Nashville: Tennessee Historical Commission, 1986.

Van West, Carroll, ed. *Tennessee Encyclopedia of History and Culture.* Nashville: Tennessee Historical Society, 1998.

Williams, John Hoyt. *Sam Houston*. New York: Promontory Press, 1993.

37

Sarah (Ridley) Buchanan

FRONTIER WOMAN OF INTUITION AND INITIATIVE

THIS BRAVE HEROINE of the frontier settlement at Fort Nashborough in Middle Tennessee during the 1780s and 1790s was noted for her intuition and initiative in the face of real danger from hostile native Americans of the Creek, Cherokee and Shawnee tribes.

Teenager Sarah Ridley had moved with her family in the momentous, highly perilous trek from the Watauga region on the Holston River in East Tennessee in 1779-80, led by Colonel John Donelson and Colonel James Robertson.

The settlers who huddled together in the dozen or so forts which encompassed Fort Nashborough on the Cumberland river (the site of present-day Nashville) faced danger at every turn and they were compelled to work the small plots around their log cabins with guns at their side.

Even to venture a short distance from the forts was ill-advised, but by necessity to obtain water and food it had to be done and women like Sarah Buchanan were in the front line.

Once, Sarah and a relative, Susan Everett, wandered into a party of heavily armed Indians as they were returning home on horseback to their Mill Creek fort about 500 yards distance.

Thinking quickly, Sarah urged Susan to imitate the position of a man of horseback and yelling furiously they raced towards the Indians, as if to indicate this was the head of a troop of militia seeking to confront the tribes.

In a panic, the Indians took to their heels and headed off leaving just as frightened Sarah and Susan enough time to make it back safely to their fort.

This incident gave Sarah the title of "the fast rider of Mill Creek" and soon after at the age of 18 she married widower Major John Buchanan, a formidable Scots-Irish frontiersman whose family had moved from Lancaster in Pennsylvania and who had served under General Andrew Pickens in the patriot militia of South Carolina.

Indeed, Major John was a kinsman of President James Buchanan, who was also born in Lancaster, Pennsylvania.

The couple lived at Buchanan's Station in Middle Tennessee and it was there that she witnessed the killing of her father-in-law at the gates of the fort by Indians, and a short time later her brother-in-law was scalped to death after being surprised by Indians, several hundred yards from the station.

Death from Indian attack was a common occurrence at this settlement and womenfolk like Sarah Buchanan had to be tough to endure.

It was a dangerous situation, but Sarah Buchanan was a woman of sturdy resolve and on another occasion, armed with a large hunting-knife, she warded off two horse thieves intent of taking the Major's two horses.

By the early 1780s, peace treaties were being successfully negotiated with the Indian tribes as more and more white settlers moved into the region requiring land.

However, warlike elements in the Cherokee, Creek and Shawnee tribes led by a militant chieftain, John Watt, still posed danger and, from a base on the Tennessee River below Chattanooga, they continued their attacks on the settlements in the Cumberland River valley region of Middle Tennessee.

Buchanan Station, four miles east of Fort Nashborough, was vulnerable to Indian attack, especially after 500 militia men in the region were stood down at the end of peace talks which some wrongfully thought would bring permanent peace.

An attack came in September, 1792 and, with only about twenty men to defend the station from an estimated 300 Creek and Cherokee Indians, Major John Buchanan feared the worst. The shortage of manpower meant they had to fire their guns often and in volleys, and very soon the ammunition ran out.

Sarah Buchanan, however, was not for giving in and, with her sister-in-law Nancy, she gathered together all the metal plates and spoons at the station and had them quickly moulded into bullets, more than three hundred in all which helped relieve a pretty desperate situation.

The women ranked as soldiers on this occasion and fired repeatedly. Other women were engaged in making bullets or creating distractions to make the besiegers believe that the fort was strongly manned.

The attack on Buchanan's Station lasted for four hours and, against all the odds, there were many more casualties on the Indian side than in the fort and the tribesmen were forced to retreat.

During the fierce fighting, it was said Sarah Buchanan aided the successful defence of the station by words and deeds, "as if life and death depended upon the efforts which she made."

Danger from Indian attack prevailed in the region until 1796, but, with enormous strength of purpose and determination, Sarah Buchanan, the most fearless of women, made sure that her homestead remained intact.

Sarah mothered 13 children and, although she had very little early education, she managed to run the home and show inspiring leadership in the most trying of circumstances.

She was of Scots-Irish Presbyterian stock, but, while she did not belong to a particular church, Sarah scrupulously kept the Sabbath and taught her children to have regard for religious duties.

Sarah died on November 23, 1831—her husband John a year later, and both are buried on the site of the old Buchanan's Station.

Sarah Buchanan's life on the American frontier is summed up by the inscription:

Oh Pilgrim Mothers, few the lyres
Your praises to prolong;
Though fame embalms the pilgrim sites
And trumpets them in song.
Yet ye were to those hearts of oak
The secret of their might;
Ye nerved the arm that hurled the stroke
In labor or in fight.
Oh, Pilgrim Mothers! though ye lie,
Perchance in graves unknown;
A memory that cannot die,
Hath claimed you for its own.

References:

Ellet, Elizabeth F. *The Women of the American Revolution.* New York: Haskell House Publishers, 1969.

Harkness, David J. "Colonial Heroines of Tennessee, Kentucky and Virginia." Compiled by University of Tennessee, 1974.

38

Mary Draper Ingles

PIONEERING WOMAN OF KENTUCKY

MARY INGLES was arguably the first white woman to reach Kentucky (or Kentucke), long before it was settled by Daniel Boone and his adventurous long hunters in the 1770s and 1780s. Indeed, Mary is claimed to be the first white bride west of the Allegheny Mountains.

Her nightmarish journey into Kentucky, then known as "the dark and bloody land," is one of the truly epic stories of the 18th century American frontier, and remarkably Mary lived to tell the tale.

Mary, of English extraction, was born in Philadelphia, Pennsylvania and had lived with her emigrant farmer husband William (they married in 1750) in the essentially Scots-Irish community at Augusta County in the Shenandoah Valley of Virginia.

Her terrible ordeal began in July, 1755 when she was taken captive by Shawnee Indians from north of the Ohio River, along with her two young sons Thomas and George during a raid on settlers at Draper's Meadows in south western Virginia, close to Roanoke, and later to be known as Blacksburg.

William Ingles was working in his wheat field at the time and Mary's brother John Draper, who also lived at Draper's Meadow with his wife Bettie Robertson Draper, was away from home.

Bettie Draper spotted the Shawnee warriors first and, realising the danger, she frantically ran into the house, grabbed her sleeping infant and tried to escape through the back. But an Indian grappled with her and broke her right arm, causing her to drop the child. She again picked up the child, and attempted another escape, but she was captured and the infant was killed.

The Ingles and Draper homes and barns were destroyed and both Mary and Bettie Draper were taken captive, along with their children, to the Shawnee village of Chillicothe in Ohio.

Bettie Draper, with her wounded arm, suffered a lot of torture from her captors, who killed two of the men, but at Chillicothe she was adopted into the family of an old Indian chief and treated with kindness until she tried to escape.

She was instantly apprehended and sentenced to burn at the stake, but the Indian chief ordered compassion and Bettie was forced to remain in the village, where she taught the women to cook and sew, and she nursed the sick so well that the Indians regarded her with special affection.

Six years later, her husband John Draper discovered her location, after a long and exhaustive search and he had to pay a large ransom for her release. The couple returned to Draper's Meadows and Bettie mothered seven children.

The plight of Mary Ingles, however, was somewhat different, for on the third night of her captivity by the Indians, she gave birth to a daughter. Mary was 23 at the time and so strong and robust was she that the day after the birth she was able to mount a horse and, with the baby in her arms, head off with her captors.

A number of other settlers were brutally massacred in the Draper's Meadow attack which came at the start of the nine-year French-Indian War. They included Colonel James Patton, a pioneer Scots-Irish frontiersman.

Mary was separated from her sister-in-law and, along with five others, she was taken by the Indians to the Big Bone Lick area on the south side of the Ohio River in Boone County, Eastern Kentucky.

Her two little boys were taken from her. George, the younger one who was only two when captured, died, but Thomas, who was four, stayed with the Indians for thirteen years until he was finally ransomed by his father and brought home.

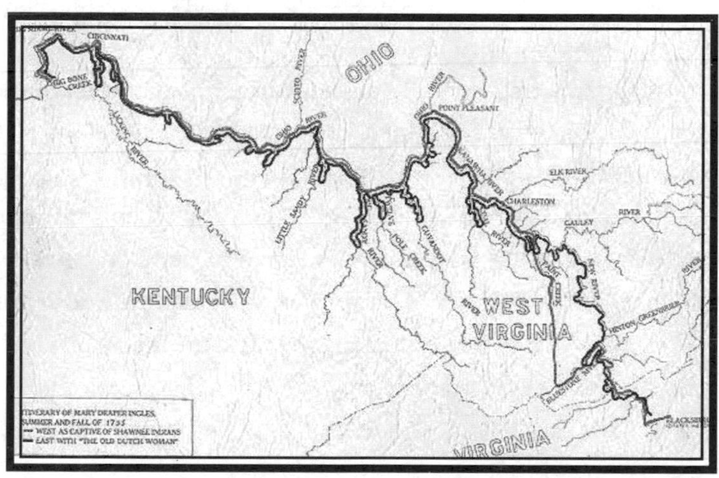

Mary Draper Ingle's Journey

The gray line shows her movement west as a captive of the Shawnee Indians, and the black line shows her return east with "the old Dutch woman." The entire trip took place in the summer and fall of 1755.

Mary somehow managed to escape along with an elderly Dutch woman who had been captured by the Indians near Fort Duquesne (Pittsburgh) in Pennsylvania. She left her baby daughter behind on the Indian settlement, in a bark cradle, realising there was no chance of a successful escape if the child was brought with them.

The pair carried only a blanket and tomahawk each and desperately they began wandering in the forests, in the forlorn but not impossible hope (as it turned out!) of making it back home.

The hardships they encountered were extreme, with the night frost penetrating through their limbs in the dark and dank wilderness. They were forced to sleep on the ground, in hollow logs and some times in deserted cabins.

For food, they ate wild grapes, roots, black walnuts, and, very occasionally, turnips and corn located on abandoned cabin plots. The pangs of hunger were almost unbearable.

They headed in a north-westerly direction towards the Kanawha River in present-day West Virginia which would have brought them, close to West Virginia and they were the first white women to enter what is now the state of Kentucky.

It was a lonely trek over 43 days and an estimated seven hundred miles, and during the ordeal Mary's elderly Dutch companion became totally worn-out through the lack of food and her mind went.

The extreme deprivation brought acute tensions between the two women and the elderly Dutch woman became so crazed with hunger that she tried to kill Mary. It was a frightening and alarming experience for Mary, who decided that her best means of survival was to try and make it home on her own.

She found an old canoe, and with an improvised paddle, she managed after nightfall to cross the Ohio River.

There was still a considerable way to travel, through the bleak mountain and forest wilderness, but, eventually, after more days of trekking, Mary reached the Adam Harmon farm, about fifteen miles from her home at Draper's Meadow.

Mary's safe return home had taken a lot of good luck, and sheer guts and perseverance, but she managed to locate the search party that was sent to find her and they in turn also rescued her demented companion who was just aimlessly wandering in the woods.

Their clothes were reduced to rags and their moccasins completely worn out. They were in a pitiful condition.

It took many months to return Mary to full health, but when she was fully restored her faithful husband William Ingles moved the family to New River Bottom near the present-day city of Radford in south western Virginia.

Incredibly, Mary had four more children and she lived until she was eighty three, dying in 1815.

It had been a perilous adventure, but Mary and her husband and friends were able to make good use of the experience, after she related some of the pathways in the mountains and forests of the still largely unexplored and uninhabited Kentucky and West Virginia territories.

Interestingly, Mary Draper Ingles and Bettie Draper when they were first captured by the Shawnee Indians in 1755 were the first white persons to have reached the present site of Charleston in West Virginia.

A bronze monument erected to the memory of Mary Draper Ingles in a Radford, Virginia cemetery carries the words: "No greater exhibition of female heroism, courage and endurance are recorded in the annals of frontier history."

Mary Ingles, and indeed her sister-in-law Bettie Draper, were true pioneers of the American frontier.

References:

Clark, Thomas D. *A History of Kentucky.* Ashland, Kentucky: Jesse Stuart Foundation, 1992.

Harkness, David J. "Colonial Heroines of Tennessee, Kentucky and Virginia." Compiled by University of Tennessee, 1974.

Rouse Jr., Parke. *The Great Wagon Road.* Richmond: The Dietz Press, 1995.

Steele, Roberta Ingles and Andrew Lewis Ingles, eds. *Escape from Indian Captivity: The Story of Mary Draper Ingles and son Thomas Ingles.* 2nd ed. Radford, Virginia: Commonwealth Press, 1982.

The American frontier woman led a life of hardship. Working from sun-up to sun-down, she did as much work as any man. A few of her chores were cooking, milking, churning, sewing, washing, preserving food and mixing medicines. In addition, she carried water, chopped wood and hoed the fields - all the while caring for her husband and children.

—Brenda C. Calloway

(author of *America's First Western Frontier: East Tennessee)*

39

Hardy Women on the Front Line of American Society

MEN INVARIABLY get the credit for extending the American nation and civilising the bleak wilderness that extended from the 18th century North Carolina, Tennessee and Kentucky frontier regions beyond the Mississippi River to the territories in the direction of the Pacific Ocean which, in the 19th century, became known as The West.

The men were the ones who cleared the land, built the homes, grew the food in the fields, chased off the marauding Indian tribes with their long Kentucky rifles and set up townships where ordered, close-knit communities were established.

The men folk were not, of course, the whole story on the frontier. When America was offering free land for those prepared to take it up in the 18th and 19th centuries it was not just men who arduously trekked across the Atlantic from Europe to seize the opportunity.

Women, too, wanted to be in on the great American dream, and many staked claims for 100 acres of land and more and got it.

Some of the women were unmarried and had to continually struggle for their rights in a male-dominated society, but they were characters with nerves of steel and a determination beyond belief as they ventured into the great unknown of the vast North American continent.

They came of Scots-Irish, German, English, Dutch, Scandinavian and Scottish Highland descent. All were strong, self-reliant, resourceful, loyal and, in most cases, God-fearing.

- *Some married out on the frontier.*
- *Most accompanied husbands and parents in the hazardous journey in wooden ships across the Atlantic.*
- *Some were sisters whose parents or brothers persuaded them to make a claim for land too.*
- *Some were daughters landed as children on American soil with their parents.*
- *Some became widows when their husbands were killed in the conflicts with the Indians or in the battles of the Revolutionary War.*

When many of these hardy women folk went to the 'New World' in the early to mid-18th century, they had very few worldly possessions and with their families had to live on a very basic diet of pumpkins and potatoes until they and their husbands or fathers could grow grain and other foodstuffs.

Indeed, the very early 18th century settlers had little more than wild fruits, berries, game and fish to live on. And they made a primitive porridge out of Indian corn.

Life for women on the American frontier was continuously one of toil and danger, facing drudgery, and, in many cases, illness brought on early in middle age by years of physical and mental fatigue.

But their experiences did create very strong, independent and resourceful personalities, and the tough characteristics and survival inheritances that they brought with them from the 'Old World' did equip them for the perils which they faced, and allowed them to turn adversity into situations that were ultimately beneficial to their calling in life.

Women of the 18th century period on the American frontier were conditioned to lives of constant labour, and they certainly lived up to the designation of "Janes-of-all trades", as they coped with the perennial chores of the home, and on the farm lands that they cultivated.

The earliest of the European immigrant settlers in colonial

American of the 16th century were male. Very few women ventured across the Atlantic on the exploratory trips into Virginia and the other eastern seaboard regions. It was considered much too dangerous a place for women.

Even by 1625, men in Virginia outnumbered women seven to one which made it very difficult for the males to find partners for marriage. However, by the 18th century, the large influx of European settlers in the eastern seaboard and Appalachian regions happily resulted in a more even spread of the sexes.

The 18th century settlers, particularly of a Scots-Irish hue, brought their own flax seeds to plant and grow for linen-making in the one-room log cabin homes. There was the complex, laborious process of preparation, bleaching, spinning and weaving and the women were in the forefront of this work.

During harvest time and threshing day (normally a popular neighbourhood event in frontier communities) women and the older girls in the family helped out in the fields when they could, but they also had to prepare in the household for both the noon-day and the evening meals.

In many of the early American frontier settlements, clothes worn by all of the family were home-made, with deerskin and leather breaches generally the garb of the men and the boys, and when woolen and linsey yarn was not available, the women and girls had to use the same materials as the males.

The linsey gown was spun and dyed and fashioned together by the women themselves and for head gear they worn sunbonnets.

The Scots-Irish of the Carolina back country wore clothes in a style that was different from the English settlers in the region, with some Anglican missionaries claiming the garb of the women was "scandalously revealing."

For most of the time in the very mild South Carolina climate the men wore only a thin shirt and a pair of breeches or trousers and very often they went about barelegged and barefooted. Some of the young women, also bareheaded, barelegged and barefooted, wore only a thin shift and petticoat in the warm summer and autumn climes.

Married women, however, dressed more modestly in long homespun dresses, with woolen shawls draped across their head and shoulders. Elderly women wore heavy hooded bonnets and coarse shoes.

Descriptions, however, of how the settlers dressed varied from region to region, and depended on the prosperity or otherwise of a region.

For "Sunday-go-to-Meeting" garb, the clothes had a distinctive look, as an accurate historical recollection of dress from the 1770s-1780s Charlotte-Waxhaw Scots-Irish settlements of the Carolinas back country reveals.

"The old country folk were dressed with their usual neatness, especially the women, whose braw garments brought from Ireland were carefully preserved, most merely from thrift, but as a memorial of the green isle of their birth.

"They wore fur hats, with narrow rims and large feathers, their hair neatly braided, hanging over their shoulders, or fastened by the black ribbon bound around their heads. The handsome dress of silk or chintze—a mixture of wool and flax—or of Irish calico, fitted each wearer with marvelous neatness, and the collar or ruffles of linen white as snow, with the high-heeled shoes, completed their attire.

"It was always a mystery to the dames who had spent their lives or many years in the country, how the gowns of the late-comers could be made to fit so admirably. Their own, in spite of every effort, showing a sad deficiency in this respect.

"The secret of the difference probably lay in the circumstance that the females from the old country wore stays well fortified with whale bone.

"The men on their part, appeared not less adorned in their coats of fine broadcloth, with their breeches, large knee buckles of pure silver and hose of various colors. They wore shoes fastened with a large strap secured with a buckle or white topped boots leaving exposed three or four inches of the hose from the knee downward.

"It must be acknowledged that this people, so strict in their religious opinions, were somewhat remarkable in their fondness for dress. They considered it highly irreverent to appear at church not clad in their best attire, and though when engaged in labor during the week, they conformed to the custom of their neighbors, wearing the coarse homespun of their own manufacture.

"On the Sabbath it was touching to see how much of decent pride there was in the exhibition of the fine clothes brought from beyond the seas."

On the American frontier, the more adult women were lumbered with the task of carrying, over a considerable distance from the river creek to the log cabin home, heavy pails of water. The family laundry had to be done by hand at the stream, in all weathers on an almost daily basis and fresh water in wooden buckets from the wells had to be borne to the log cabins.

Women scoured the land for anything burnable on the home fire and, if firewood was not available, they were forced to rely on dried twigs, tufts of grass and old corn cobs.

Garden crops which added to a staple diet were attended to by the women and they also produced a variety of food, clothing and household utensils to sell locally in the market places for very necessary income.

Teenage girls and the older children had to assist with the work in the fields, dropping seed corn and gathering flax, which they later hatchelled, spun and wove. They were adept at the loom and with the needle in the cottage industries that abounded in the back country settlements.

Care of the vegetable garden and the dairying was also a women's chore as well as looking after poultry, and they also engaged in the making of sugar from maple sap.

On a more business footing, there were women on the frontier who enterprisingly and with considerable courage ran village shops and wayside taverns. And, of course, midwifery and nursing had to be an inevitable calling for some of the women in the various localities.

Child-birthing, with only the most basic facilities and medical help in the wilds of the frontier, was a risky operation for both the mother and the child. But the women of the settlements could always be relied upon to help each other and before and during a birth the necessary precautions, within the very limited means available to protect life, were taken.

Infant mortality was significantly higher on the 18th century American frontier than on the more settled eastern seaboard communities, with no hospitals and few if any doctors, but remarkably the majority of children born in the white settlements survived.

Very often, the mothers were "doctors" to their own children and the women took care, if they were not stricken down themselves, of other members of the family when they were infected by smallpox, malaria, pneumonia, cholera, pleurisy and ague (the frontier fever).

It was generally accepted in the early American settlement years that the proper place for a woman of good family and respectability was at home, but to survive in frontier communities everyone had to be adaptable, even the female members of the family.

They all had to work and work hard, and it was accepted that a high degree of managerial skills marked out the women of the frontier!

The work extended, in many instances to tending the livestock and slaughtering of even the largest of animals. British travellers in the 18th century American back country were shocked to see females fell animals with an axe and engage in the hard labour of forest and land clearing.

It was noted that back country women were not only "up to their elbows in housewifery, but were busy with what other white ethnic cultures took to be man's work."

Women had few if any legal rights in 18th century American frontier society and marriage was considered a practical social and economic necessity in the harsh and far from accommodating environment for female rights.

Indeed, the conservative view, prevalent mainly in the Southern states, was that the woman's place was in the home, under-written by the Old Testament Biblical philosophy which scrupulously upheld the traditional concept of male supremacy in the family and in the wider community.

However, the legal and social conditions of women in some states did improve considerably by the mid-19th century, permitting them to sue in courts, make contracts, exercise full control over their personal affairs and retain custody of their children in a matrimonial dispute.

When a husband was missing from home for a long period while engaged in militia battles and presumed dead, the wives were permitted to re-marry. If the husband did re-appear and there was existential bigamy, the wife was permitted to choose between spouses.

Conditions were no different for women in the north, particularly in the North-West Territory where the new lands of Illinois were being open up in the late 18th century.

It was said, however, that the support system provided to the men by the resolute and fiercely loyal women was a crucial factor in ensuring the survival of the new life in the raw settlements of Illinois.

Women may not have enjoyed equal rights to men in holding civic office, but their share of the work load in sustaining a home was at least on a par.

In 1896, eminent Scotch-Irish historian the Rev Dr. Henry C. McCook, of Philadelphia, describing those early frontier women's efforts, said they had to be physician and surgeon, as well as attending to all their own work.

The onerous duties and burdens of home-making, and child-caring, he said, largely fell on their shoulders.

McCook, in *Scotch-Irish Women Pioneers*, wrote: "There was neither bedstead, nor stool, nor chair, nor bucket, nor domestic comfort. But such as could be carried on pack horses and the Conestoga wagon through the wilderness. Two rough boxes, one attached to the other served as the table, two kegs for seats and so on.

"Having committed themselves to God in family worship they spread their bed on the floor and slept soundly until morning. Some times they had no bread for weeks together, but they had plenty of pumpkins and potatoes and all the necessities of life.

"The earliest settlers, of course, did not have the luxuries of pumpkins and potatoes, to begin their culinary duties therewith. They had in sooth to invent a cuisine. Everything must be found anew.

"The wild fruits, wild berries and wild game and the fish of the New World were utilised. Indian corn was a new cereal to these Ulster housewives, but it had to be wrought into the primitive menu, mush and milk!

"It was a novel sort of porridge for our grandames but they learned to make it. Cooking was not the only sphere that solicited her faculty. The pioneer woman had to invent a pharmacopoeia.

"Wounds and sickness came, and must be cared for. The forest was full of healing herbs—and, perhaps, our octogenarian members still have recollection of ginseng and snakeroot teas and slippery elm poultices, and the like.

"The frontier woman had to be physician and surgeon, trained in nursing and apothecary, all in one, and often supplied the patient, too in her own person. In times of personal sickness and during the illness of children, the strain upon women thus situated must have been intense.

"Such a life, indeed, developed self-reliance; fertility of resources, strong and independent characters, but many fell under the grievous strain and thus became veritable martyrs

"In these humble log huts began the work of home building, constructing that prime factor of all strong and good social order, the family. The family is the unity of society, the true basis of the best civilisation and the pioneer family building woman was the chief architect.

"The husband indeed must fend and fight for wife and weans, for steading and glebe; he must shoot game, and chop down trees and clear up fields and plant grain, but the duty and burden of home-making must fall upon the wife and mother. And well our Scotch-Irish pioneers did their work."

Often, the frontier women had to work in the fields barefoot when moccasins were not available and, when it came to building the log cabins and churches, they helped their men-folk make a clearing in the forest by cutting down the trees.

An example of this challenge was the immigrant women from Co Antrim in the north of Ireland who helped their men-folk build Timber Ridge Presbyterian Church at Lexington in the Shenandoah Valley of Virginia in the early 1750s.

These women of Ulster extraction did 10-mile trips on horseback, through hostile Indian country to carry sand used for "lyme" in the church's construction.

During the 18th century years of American settlement, women were traditionally kept in the background of church life, with the preaching, teaching and decision-making essentially a male preserve.

Female clerics were unheard of and frowned upon by the church establishments in every denomination.

Increasingly, however, by the 19th century, women in the American back country territories were given an active role in church-support agencies providing financial backing for mission work, at home and abroad. But the pulpit remained out of bounds for females in most American churches until the mid-20th century and even today this view holds sway with some congregations in Appalachian back country regions.

Many frontier women had to survive stark loneliness and for months and even years they bore the burden of looking after the household chores and the constant care of the children.

The loneliness and mental anguish for the women was most acute when the men were away for long periods, either working the land from dawn to dusk, hunting in the forests, on business and trading commitments, or soldiering far from their homes in the locally-recruited militia units in the battles of the Revolutionary War and in the expeditions conducted against hostile Indian tribes.

Stout means of defence were a very necessary requirement on the frontier forts and townships, and very often the women fought alongside the men when they were in a tight spot.

Brandishing a long Kentucky rifle with accuracy and determination at a stockade under siege from Indians was not solely confined to males and the tales of legendary heroines gallantly defending their home or fort and children are an integral part of frontier folklore.

On the frontier, the white European settlers faced cold and bitter winters and hot, dust bowl summers, swarms of crickets, insects of all descriptions, the wildest of animals, and tornadoes which often ripped their wooden homes apart and left them vulnerable.

The Rev Henry C. McCook, vividly describing the character and work ethic of the frontier women, said: "Stalwart of frame, no doubt they were, with muscles hardened under the strain of toil, hale and hearty, vigorous and strong, able to wield the axe against the trunk of a forest monarch or the head of an intruding savage; to aid their husbands and fathers to plow and plant, to reap and mow, to rake and bind and gather.

"They could wield the scutching knife or hackling comb upon flaxen stocks and fibres, as well as the rod of rebuke upon the back of a refractory child. They could work the treadle of a little spinning wheel, or swing the circumference of the great one. They could brew and bake, make and mend, sweep and scrub, rock the cradle and rule the household."

John Anderson, son of a late 18th century Scots-Irish settler in the Holston River region of East Tennessee, colloquially detailed some customs of the early pioneer families.

Anderson recalled: "Their manner and dress was generally pleasant and agreeable to themselves. Strict degree of temperance prevailed throughout this newly settled part of the country.

"At the time, the dress of the women was hunting shirts and often leather britches and 'mockquesons' (sic) and when they went abroad they often neatly fringed with various colors and the sleeves neatly plaited.

"The women dressed commonly in a short gown and other clothes were plain and loose. No lacing was seen in that day. They appeared in a general way to enjoy fine health and great strength and many of them were beautiful. Their marriages were performed by Presbyterian ministers, whose fee was merely that which was commonly offered them.

"The people of that time appeared clean and neat in their houses. Their table was most frequently furnished with cornbread, meat, butter and milk. There was no coffee or tea made in those days except of a domestic kind. There were few or no doctors as there was but little business for them, and not sufficient money to pay them, for their attendance.

"There were little courts of justice in the country for some considerable length of time, but very few disputes and, of course, no law suits. They in a general way appeared cheerful and happy when they were not disturbed by Indians."

Many frontier women were married in their early teens and had families running into double figures by the time they were 30. Some never reached middle age, worn out with the incessant struggle to keep the family intact and make ends meet as their husbands worked for long hours and little financial return on the bleak and highly dangerous frontier lands.

Very often, it was difficult to distinguish between a young mother and her teenage daughters in physical attributes and looks, such was the short age span between them.

There were always fewer women than men, of course, on the American frontier and this resulted in very short courtships and hurried marriages, nearly always conducted by a church ceremony.

Arranged marriages for the benefit of land and property acquirements were not an uncommon feature of the frontier, such was the need, and perhaps greed to add to one's estate.

No women regardless of their looks or society ranking were single for too long and spinsters were a very rare species in most communities. The husbands were nearly always older than their wives, very often 20 and 30 years separating them. Bachelors were much more common than spinsters in frontier communities.

Widows, just bereaved, had never too long to wait before again being "spoken for"; thus the large number of frontiersmen who are recorded as having several wives due to the deaths of spouses.

Having the companionship and care of a dedicated and loving wife was a very necessary requirement for men aspiring to prosperity on the American frontier, but some men had to fend for themselves as bachelors and widowers and for them it was a very lonely existence.

The Rev Charles Woodmason, an outspoken itinerant Anglican preacher who held a patronising High Church view of the non-conformist immigrants, made an interesting observation of Scots-Irish frontier settlements in the Carolinas during a tour of the Appalachian back country in the 1760s.

Woodmason said: "There is not a cabin but has ten or twelve children in it. When the boys are 18 and the girls 14 they marry—so that in many cabins you will see children—and the mother looking as young as the daughter."

Living in the bleak frontier environment, the Scots-Irish women in particular, were strong characters—self-reliant, resourceful and loyal. Devout, patient and cheerful in the midst of difficulties, they pursued with vigour the even tenor of their ways, performing with efficient diligence the duties that lay nearest them.

The elders in the church, politics and in civic society were the men, and they were the ones who took the ultimate decisions that directly affected their communities. However, the women did have considerable influence in many aspects of American frontier life, essentially in the home, in the rearing of children and in maintaining decent upright standards of life.

The contribution of the frontier women in the making of the United States of America in the 18th and early 19th century was immense and only now is it being fully recognised in this more equitable modern society where male and female rights in most instances are equal, and more readily taken for granted.

References:

Clark, Thomas D. *A History of Kentucky*. Ashland, Kentucky: Jesse Stuart Foundation, 1992.

Edmonds, Bobby F. *The Making of McCormick County*. McCormick, South Carolina: Cedar Hill Publishing, 1999.

Ellet, Elizabeth F. *The Women of the American Revolution*. New York: Haskell House Publications, 1969.*History of Augusta County*. Lexington.

Faragher, John Mack, ed. *The American Heritage: Encyclopedia of American History*. New York: Henry Holt and Company, 1998.

Fischer, David Hackett. *Albion's Seed*. New York and Oxford: Oxford University Press, 1989.

Fischer, David Hackett and James C. Kelly. *Bound Away: Virginia and the Westward Movement*. Charlottesville and London: University Press of Virginia, 2000.

Lewis, Jon E. *The Mammoth Book of the West: The Making of the American West.* London: Robinson Publications, 1996.

Timber Ridge Presbyterian Church (The Old Stone Church), Lexington, Virginia.

Williams, Samuel Cole. *History of the Lost State of Franklin.* Johnston City, Tennessee: The Overmountain Press, 1923, 1933 and 1993.

Index

BIBLIOGRAPHY

Adair, James. *Reflections of the Lifestyles and Culture of 18th Century Native American People*. London, 1770.

Boatner, Mark W. III, ed. *Encyclopedia of the American Revolution*. Mechanicsburg, Pennsylvania: Stackpole Books, 1966.

Booraem, Hendrik. *Young Hickory: The Making of Andrew Jackson*. Dallas, Texas: Taylor Publishing Company, 2001.

Bracken, Jeanne Munn, ed. *Women in the American Revolution*. Carlisle, Massachusetts: Discovery Enterprises, 1997.

Burghardt, Renie. *History's Women: The Unsung Heroines: Deborah Sampson, A Soldier of the Revolution*.

Burns, Hobert W. *The Life of Anne Calhoun Matthews*. Comer, South Carolina: Abbeville Books, 1996.

Calloway, Brenda. *America's First Western Frontier*. Johnson City: The Overmountain Press, 1989.

Clark, Thomas D. *A History of Kentucky*. Ashland, Kentucky: Jesse Stuart Foundation, 1992.

Craig, Erwin, Johnston, Davis and Owen Genealogy, 1988.

Creekmore, Betsey Beeler. *Knox County, Tennessee*.

Cruse, Katherine W. *An Amiable Woman: Rachel Jackson*. Nashville: The Ladies' Hermitage Association, 1994.

Crutchfield, James A. *Tennesseans at War*. Nashville: Rutledge Hill Press, 1987.

Davis, William C. *The American frontier: Pioneers, Settlers and Cowboys 1800-1899*. University of Oklahoma Press, 1992.

Davis, William C. *Three Roads To the Alamo*. New York: Harper Collins Publishers, 1998.

Deaderick, Lucile, ed. *Heart of the Valley: A History of Knoxville, Tennessee*. East Tennessee Historical Society, 1976.

Degregorio, William A. *The Complete Book of US Presidents.* Avenel, New Jersey: Random House Publishing, 1984.

Dykeman, Wilma. *Tennessee: A New History.* Newport, Tennessee: Wakestone Books, 1984.

Edmonds, Bobby F. *The Making of McCormick County*. McCormick, South Carolina: Cedar Hill Publishing, 1999.

Ellet, Elizabeth F. *The Women of the American Revolution*. New York: Haskell House Publications, 1850 and 1969.

Faragher, John Mack. *The American Heritage: Encyclopedia of American History*. New York: Henry Holt Incorporated, 1998.

Fischer, David Hackett. *Albion's Seed: Four British Folkways in America*. New York: Oxford University Press, 1989.

Fischer, David Hackett and James C. Kelly. *Bound Away: Virginia and the Westward Movement*. Charlottesville and London: University Press of Virginia, 2000.

Haley, James J. *Sam Houston.* Norman, Oklahoma: Oklahoma University, 2002.

Hallberg, Carl. "Women's History in Wyoming." Wyoming State Archives.

Harkness, David J. "Colonial Heroines of Tennessee, Kentucky and Virginia." Compiled by University of Tennessee, 1974.

Harper, Herbert L., ed. *Houston and Crockett : Heroes of Tennessee and Texas: an Anthology*. Nashville: Tennessee Historical Commission, 1986.

Hatley, Thomas. "Cherokee Women Farmers" from *Appalachian Frontiers: Settlement, Society and Development in the Pre-Industrial Era*. Mitchell, Robert D., ed. Lexington: University of Kentucky Press, 1991.

Harvey, Robert. *A Few Bloody Noses: The American War of Independence*. London: John Murray Limited, 2001.

History's Women: The Unsung Heroines. Lexington, Virginia: History of Augusta County.

Howard, Robert A. and E. Alvin Gerhardt Jr. *Mary Patton: Powder Maker of the Revolution.* Tennessee: Rocky Mount Historical Association, 1980.

Hurd, E. Don. *The South Carolina Up-Country.* 1981.

Kunhardt Jr., Philip B., Philip B. Kunhardt III and Peter W. Kunhardt. *The American President*. New York: Riverhead Books, 1999.

Lewis, Jon E. *The Mammoth Book of the West: The Making of the American West.* London: Robinson Publications, 1996.

Leyburn, James G. *The Scotch-Irish: A Social History.* Chapel Hill: North Carolina, The University of North Carolina Press, 1962.

Lofaro, Michael A., ed. *Davy Crockett: The Man, The Legend, The Legacy.* Knoxville: University of Tennessee Press, 1985.

Mack, Ashley. "For Christ in the Heart of Knoxville: History of Knoxville First Presbyterian Church."

McHenry, Robert, ed. *Liberty's Women*. Springfield, Massachusetts: G & C Merriam and Company, 1980.

McPherson, James M., ed. *To the Best of My Ability: The American Presidents.* New York: Dorling Kindersley Books, 2000.

Miller, Mary Montgomery. "Kate Barry." Moore, South Carolina: History of Nazareth Presbyterian Church.

Mitchell, Robert D., ed. *Appalachian Frontiers: Settlements, Society and Development in the Pre-Industrial Era*. Lexington: University of Kentucky, 1991.

Moss, Bobby Gilmer. *The Patriots of Kings Mountain.* Blacksburg, South Carolina: Scotia-Hibernia Press, 1990.

Nashville: Tennessee Historical Society Collection.

Nashville: Tennessee State Library and Archives Museum.

Nashville: The Hermitage Historical Collection.

Paris, Captain R. L., Calhoun: Georgia.

Presidents of the United States. Maryland: Coffman Publications, 1996.

Remini, Robert V. *The Life of Andrew Jackson.* New York: Penguin Books, 1988.

Rothrock, Mary U., ed. *The French- Broad-Holston Country: A History of Knox County, Tennessee.* Knoxville: East Tennessee Historical Society, 1972.

Rouse Jr., Parke. *The Great Wagon Road.* Richmond: The Dietz Press, 1995.

Salley, A. S., "The Grandfather of John C. Calhoun." *South Carolina Historical and Genealogical Magazine*, 1938.

Sawyer, Susan. *More Than Petticoats: Remarkable Tennessee Women*. Helena, Montana: TwoDot, 2000.

Sketch on the Life and Imprisonment of Mary (Neely) Spears. Nashville: Tennessee State Library and Archives.

South Carolina Gazette (South Carolina State Archives, Columbia). February 23, 1760 and March 1-8, 1760.

Steele, Roberta Ingles and Andrew Lewis Ingles, eds. *Escape from Indian Captivity: The Story of Mary Draper Ingles and son Thomas Ingles*. 2nd ed. Radford, Virginia: Commonwealth Press, 1982.

Taylor, Oliver. *Historic Sullivan: Tennessee.* Johnson City, Tennessee: Overmountain Press, 1988.

The Wild West. Warner Books.

Thom, James Alexander. *From Sea to Shining Sea.* New York: Ballentine Books, 1984.

Timber Ridge Presbyterian Church (The Old Stone Church), Lexington, Virginia.

Trefousse, Hans L. *Andrew Johnson.* New York: W. W. Norton and Company, 1989.

Van West, Carroll, ed. *Tennessee Encyclopedia of History and Culture*. Nashville: Tennessee Historical Society, 1998.

Waring, Alice Noble. *The Fighting Elder: Andrew Pickens.* Columbia, South Carolina, 1962.

Williams, John Hoyt. *Sam Houston*. New York: Promontory Press, 1993.

Williams, Samuel Cole. *History of the Lost State of Franklin*. Johnston City, Tennessee: The Overmountain Press, 1923, 1933 and 1993.

Wood, Mayme Parrot. *Hitch Hiking Along the Holston River.* Nashville: Richland Press, 1964.

Author's Acknowledgements

Adamson, Councillor Dr. Ian (Belfast, Northern Ireland)

Cook, Brenton (Greenville, South Carolina)

Crabtree, Larry (Huntsville, Alabama)

Croston, Andy (Greenville, South Carolina)

Graham, Stephen (Co Armagh, Northern Ireland)

Henderson, Cherel (East Tennessee Historical Society. Knoxville, Tennessee)

Irwin, John Rice (Museum of Appalachia. Norris, Tennessee)

Lowry, Gillian (Belfast, Northern Ireland)

Lowry, Dr. Samuel (Belfast, Northern Ireland)

Martin, Bev (Huntsville, Alabama)

Moss, Dr. Bobby (Blacksburg, South Carolina)

Shepherd, Paula (Greenville, South Carolina)

Staff at the Calvin M. McClung Historical Collection (Knoxville, Tennessee)

Tennessee State Library and Archives (Nashville, Tennessee)

Pictures and Illustrations

Crabtree, Larry (Huntsville, Alabama)

Edmonds, Bobby F. (McCormick, South Carolina)

Guzzi, Tony (Curator at The Hermitage Museum. Nashville, Tennessee)

Hume, Dr. David (Larne, Co Antrim)

Wright, David (Nashville, Tennessee)—*Gateway to the West* (Cumberland Gap National Historic Park) cover, *The Blue Belt* (From the collection of Norm & Toodie Burke) p. 42, *Moutain Lamb* (From the collection of Henry & Gail Butler) p. 94, *White Rose* (From the collection of Norm & Toodie Burke) p. 101, *Ahnawake* p. 114, *The Mountaineer* p. 174

Page vi: A map of the British Isles. *Page x:* Women were prominent in the movement by frontiersmen Daniel Boone and Scots-Irish pioneers along the Wilderness Road through the Cumberland Gap into Kentucky in the 1770s. Painting by Claude Regnier after the painting by George Caleb Bingham. Published by agreement with and courtesy of the Missouri Historical Society. *Page 8:* The inside of a typical frontier log cabin.

Billy Kennedy viewing *Gateway to the West* at the Cumberland Gap National Historic Park in Middlesboro, KY (painting by David Wright).

About the Author

BILLY KENNEDY has now written eight books in the popular Scots-Irish Chronicles which focus on the 18th century American frontier settlements. This latest work, *Women of the Frontier*, vividly highlights the outstanding contributions and enormous sacrifices made by hardy and courageous womenfolk (not only of Scots-Irish origin, but also of other European emigrant ethnicity and native American culture). Life was not an easy load for these frontier woman, but possesing unusual character and fortitude, most of them managed to surmount the adversities that came their way on a daily basis.

Billy Kennedy lives in Co Armagh, Northern Ireland, and has been a leading journalist there for the past 30 years. He has occupied the roles of Religious Affairs and Cultural Correspondent, Political Correspondant, Assistant Editor, and News Editor with the Belfast *News Letter* (the primary morning newspaper in Northern Ireland and oldest English-written newspaper in the world).

Billy has also worked for other media outlets in Northern Ireland and in other parts of the United Kingdom. On his regular visits to the United States, Billy lectures on the subject of the Scots-Irish diaspora at universities, colleges, historical and genealogical societies and public authorities in cities and towns of the south eastern American states. His other main interests are soccer and American country music. Billy is married and has one fully-grown daughter.

Billy Kennedy can be contacted at:

49, Knockview Drive,
Tandragee, Craigavon, Northern Ireland BT62 2BH.
E-mail address: billykennedy@fsmail.net

The Scots-Irish Chronicles

by BILLY KENNEDY

The Scots-Irish in the Hills of Tennessee
(First published 1995)

This book centred in Tennessee is the definite story of how the American frontier of the late 18th century was advanced and the indomitable spirit of the Scots-Irish shines though on every page. From the Great Smoky Mountain region to the Cumberland Plateau and the Mississippi delta region, the Scots-Irish created a civilisation out of a wilderness. The inheritance they left was hard-won, but something to cherish. The careers of Tennessean Presidents Andrew Jackson, James Knox Polk and Andrew Johnson and state luminaries Davy Crockett and Sam Houston are catalogued in the book.

The Scots-Irish in the Shenandoah Valley
(First published 1996)

The beautiful Shenandoah Valley alongside the majestic backdrop of the Blue Ridge Mountains of Virginia is the idyllic setting for the intriguing story of a brave resolute people who tamed the frontier. The Ulster-Scots (Scots-Irish) were a breed of people who could move mountains. They did this literally with their bare hands in regions like the Shenandoah Valley, winning the day for freedom and liberty of conscience in the United States. In the Shenandoah Valley, the Scots-Irish led the charge for the American patriots in the Revolutionary War and for the Confederates in the Civil War a century later.

The Scots-Irish in the Carolinas
(First published 1997)

The Piedmont areas of the Carolinas, North and South, were settled by tens of thousands of Scots-Irish Presbyterians in the second half of the 18th century. Some moved down the Great Wagon Road from Pennsylvania, others headed to the up-country after arriving at the port of Charleston. The culture, political heritage and legacy of the Scots-Irish so richly adorned the fabric of American life and the Carolinas was an important homeland for many of these people. It was also the launching pad for the long trek westwards to new lands and the fresh challenge of the expanding frontier.

The Scots-Irish in Pennsylvania-Kentucky
(First Published 1998)

Pennsylvania and Kentucky are two American states settled primarily at opposite ends of the 18th century by Ulster-Scots Presbyterians, yet this book details how the immigrant trail blended in such diverse regions. William Penn and the Quaker community encouraged the European settlers to move in large numbers to the colonial lands of Pennsylvania from the beginning of the 18th century and the Scots-Irish were the earliest settlers to set up homes in cities like Philadelphia and Pittsburgh. Kentucky, established as a state in 1792, was pioneered by Ulster-Scots families who moved through the Cumberland Gap and down the Wilderness Road with explorer Daniel Boone.

Faith and Freedom: The Scots-Irish in America
(First published 1999)

A common thread runs through Pennsylvania, Virginia, North Carolina, South Carolina, Tennessee, New Hampshire, West Virginia,

Georgia, Kentucky, Alabama and other neighbouring states—that of a settlement of people who had firmly set their faces on securing for all time—their Faith and Freedom. This inspirational journey of the Scots-Irish Presbyterian settlers details how they moved the American frontier to its outer limits, founding log cabin churches that were to spiral the message of the gospel and establishing schools, which were to expand into some of the foremost educational institutions in the United States.

Heroes of the Scots-Irish in America
(First published in 2000)

Heroism was a distinct characteristic of the 18th century Scots-Irish immigrants and the raw courage shown by these dogged determined people in very difficult circumstance helped make the United States great. Forging a civilisation out of a wilderness was a real challenge for the Ulster settlers and how well they succeeded in moulding a decent law-abiding society, from the eastern seaboard states, through the Appalachian region into the south to Texas and beyond. The Scots-Irish heroes and heroines have become enshrined in American history, not just as Presidents, statesmen, soldiers and churchmen, but many plain ordinary citizens whose quiet, unselfish deeds were worthy of note, and a shining example to others.

The Making of America: How the Scots-Irish Shaped a Nation
(First published 2001)

In establishing of the United States, the Scots-Irish were one of the most highly influential groups, both in the signing of the American Declaration of Independence on July 4, 1776 and in the Revolutionary War which followed. This group of dedicated stalwarts, whose families emigrated to America from the Irish province of Ulster throughout the 18th century were resolute and uncompromising champions of the movement for American independence. Bitter experience of religious discrimination and economic deprivation in their Scottish and Ulster homelands gave impetus to the Scots-Irish throwing off the shackles of the old order when they moved to the American colonies and opened up the great frontier lands. The Scots-Irish were in the vanguard of American patriot involvement on all fronts of the Revolutionary War, but it was on the frontier that they made their most significant contribution. Quite uniquely as a people they rose to the awesome challenge of the American frontier—its danger, its inaccessibility and its sheer enormity.

*These books are available from authorised booksellers in the United Kingdom, the United States and the Republic of Ireland or direct from the publishers in Belfast (Northern Ireland) and Greenville (South Carolina).

Scots-Irish Lectures

(delivered by author Billy Kennedy in the United States 1994-2004)

TENNESSEE:

- Middle Tennessee, State University Murfreesboro.
- East Tennessee State University, Johnson City.
- East Tennessee Historical Society, Knoxville.
- Tennessee First Families Reunion (2000), Knoxville
- Belmont University, Nashville.
- Maryville College, Blount County.
- King's Presbyterian College, Bristol.
- University of Tennessee, Chattanooga.
- Tennessee State University, Chattanooga.
- The Hermitage, Nashville.
- Chattanooga Historical Society.
- Barnes and Noble Store, Chattanooga.
- Scottish Association, Knoxville.
- Zion Presbyterian Church, Columbia, Maury County.
- Library, Greeneville.
- Jefferson County Historical Society in Courthouse, Dandridge
- Courthouse, Newport
- Sullivan County Genealogical Society, Kingsport.
- Rotary Club, Rogersville
- Rotary Club, Morristown.
- Franklin Historical Society (Franklin Episcopal Church)
- Museum of Appalachia, Norris.
- Smith County Historical and Genealogical Society, Carthage.
- Cumberland and Bledsoe County Genealogical and Historical Society, Crossville.
- Louden County Historical Society, Leinore City.
- Jonesboro Visitors Centre and Museum.
- Tolahoma Historical Society in Tolahoma Methodist Church
- Sycamore Shoals State Historic Park, Elizabethton.
- Highland Presbyterian Church, Maryville.
- Davis -Kidd Book Store, Nashville.
- Gallatin Historical Society (Palace Theatre).
- Memphis Historical and Genealogical Society.
- Maury County Archives, Columbia

VIRGINIA :

- Richmond Historical Society.
- Museum of American Frontier Culture, Staunton.
- Ferrum College.
- Grayson County Historical Society, Independence.
- Roanoke Historical Society
- Abingdon Historical Society
- The Bookery, Lexington.
- Woodrow Wilson Birthplace and Museum, Staunton.
- Book Store, Charlottesville
- Harrisonburg-Rockingham County Historical Society, Harrisonburg.
- South West Virginia Genealogical Society, Roanoke

KENTUCKY:

- Berea College, Berea.
- Cumberland Gap National Park, Middlesboro
- Harrodsburg Historical Society (Harrodsburg Historical Rooms)
- Lexington-La Fayette County Historical Museum (Lexington Public Library Theatre)
- Landmark Association, Bowling Green (Kentucky Building).
- Louisville Genealogical Society (Louisville Auditorium).

SOUTH CAROLINA :

- Clemson University.
- McCormick County Historical Society.
- Donalds Historical Society, Boonesborough
- Greenville Presbyterian Church (Donalds-Boonesborough Historical Society).
- Gaffney College.
- Kings Mountain National Military Park.
- Erskine Theological College.
- Honea Path School, Donalds.
- Union Historical and Genealogical Society (University of South Carolina Auditorium).

NORTH CAROLINA:

- Catawba Valley Highland Games, Charlotte.
- Charlotte Historical Society (South County Regional Library)
- Historical Society, Franklin.
- Andrew Jackson Centre, Waxhaw.
- Appalachian Conference, Boone.
- Historical Society, Waynesville.
- Kirk of Kildaire Presbyterian Church, Cary, Raleigh (Scottish Organisation of the Triangle,

Ulster-Scots Association of America and Wake County Geneological Society)

PENNSYLVANIA :

- Scotch-Irish Society of the United States, Philadelphia
- Elizabethton College.
- Donegal Presbyterian Church, Lancaster County.
- First Pittsburgh Presbyterian Church.
- Historical Cultural Centre, Winter's House, Elizabethton.

ALABAMA :

- Tennessee Valley Historical Society, Huntsville
- North East Alabama Historical Society, Gadsden.
- Birmingham Historical and Genealogical Society (Birmingham down-town Library)

GEORGIA :

- Funk Heritage Centre, Reinhart College, Waleski.
- Historical Genealogical Group, La Grange.
- Dalton Historical Society.
- Stone Mountain Highland Games, Atlanta.

WASHINGTON DC:

- Northern Ireland Bureau reception in Washington.